# BRAVE NEW WORLD ORDER

# BRAVE NEW WORLD ORDER

*Must We Pledge Allegiance?*

## Jack Nelson-Pallmeyer

ORBIS BOOKS

**Maryknoll, New York 10545**

24629960

The Catholic Foreign Mission Society of America (Maryknoll) recruits and trains people for overseas missionary service. Through Orbis Books, Maryknoll aims to foster the international dialogue that is essential to mission. The books published, however, reflect the opinions of their authors and are not meant to represent the official position of the society.

Copyright © 1992 by Jack Nelson-Pallmeyer

Published by Orbis Books, Maryknoll, NY 10545

Manufactured in the United States of America

**Library of Congress Cataloging-in-Publication Data**

Nelson-Pallmeyer, Jack.
    Brave new world order : must we pledge allegiance? / Jack Nelson-Pallmeyer.
        p. cm.
    Includes bibliographical references and index.
    ISBN 0-88344-785-1 (paper)
    1. United States—Foreign relations—1989-  2. Christianity and international affairs.  3. Persian Gulf War, 1991—Religious aspects.  4. Persian Gulf War, 1991—Influence.  5. World politics—1985-1995.  6. Security, International.  I. Title.
E881.N45   1992
327.73—dc20                                      91-37238
                                                    CIP

# Contents

Introduction      **vii**

**1. Brave New Third-World Order**      **1**
A Third-World Perspective on Who "Won" the Cold
     War    3
Third-World Coverup    5
Wealth Transfers and Third-World Poverty    7
Conclusion    17

**2. Brave New First-World Order**      **18**
Domestic Hunger and Poverty    19
Economic Decline    23
Conclusion    30

**3. National Security State Doctrine and the New World
Order**      **33**
Dangerous Features    34
Conclusion    41

**4. The U.S. National Security State**      **42**
Formation of a National Security State    42
Disturbing Signs of a U.S. National Security State    46
Conclusion    53

**5. Policing the Brave New World Order**      **55**
Military or Economic Strength: A Choice    57
The "Threat of Peace"    59
The Search for Enemies    61
Shift of Focus to the Third World    62

v

New Support for Low-Intensity Conflict    66
Conclusion    69

6. **The Gulf War and the Brave New World Order**    **71**
Opportunity Lost    72
Winners and Losers    81
Conclusion    92

7. **Environmental Disorder in the Brave New World Order**  **94**
Signs of Environmental Crisis    95
The Environmental Crisis and Third-World Poverty    98
Environmental Destruction and the National Security
     State    102
Conclusion    112

8. **Mark, Jesus, and the Kingdom: Confronting World
Orders, Old and New**    **114**
Competing Gospels: The Confrontation with Empire    115
The Conflict with Religious Authorities    118
Alternative Community as Gospel Imperative    124
Competing Spirits: Overcoming Destructive Myths    125
Obstacles to Discipleship    128
Conclusion    132

9. **The Church, the Gulf War, and the New World Order**    **133**
The Church and the Gulf War    136
A Gospel-Informed Agenda    142
Conclusion    155

**Notes**    **159**

**Index**    **170**

# Introduction

*John also laughed, but for another reason—laughed for pure joy. "O brave new world," he repeated. "O brave new world that has such people in it. Let's start at once."*

*"You have a most peculiar way of talking sometimes," said Bernard, staring at the young man in perplexed astonishment. "And anyhow, hadn't you better wait till you actually see the new world?"*

—Aldous Huxley, *Brave New World*

"The liberation of Kuwait has begun." With these words on January 16, 1991, White House spokesman Marlin Fitzwater announced the beginning of a massive U.S.-led military action against Iraq. U.S. citizens, prior to the January offensive, were evenly divided over use of military force to resolve the Gulf crisis. Many supported internationally coordinated economic sanctions and other diplomatic initiatives to force an Iraqi withdrawal from Kuwait.

But there was also opposition to military escalation of the crisis which found particular expression in the religious community. Eighteen church leaders issued a common statement declaring that "war is not the answer" following a December visit to the Middle East. "It is entirely possible," the religious leaders warned, "that war in the Middle East will destroy everything. No cause will be served, no justice secured. War will not liberate Kuwait," the statement continued, "it will destroy it. War will not save us from weapons of mass destruction, it will unleash them. War will not establish regional stability, it will inflame the entire Middle East. War will not resolve long-standing conflicts, it will explode them wider and deeper."[1]

After the U.S.-led military offensive began on January 16, President George Bush's popularity soared, meaningful public debate ceased, and criticism from most church leaders was muffled. Flags and yellow ribbons appeared almost everywhere, including in many churches. The war in the Middle East became the most popular war in U.S. history. Polls showed President Bush with a ninety percent approval rating, the highest rating for any president in U.S. history, as the war came to a swift end.

The popularity of the war was linked to its apparent success. A U.S.-led coalition using massive military force had needed only six weeks to "liberate Kuwait" and to decimate what had been projected as a formidable enemy. More important, despite the involvement of hundreds of thousands of U.S. soldiers, the United States suffered fewer than two hundred casualties. This compared to an estimated 100,000 Iraqi soldiers killed. U.S. military leaders were jubilant. The nation had apparently overcome its bondage to the "Vietnam syndrome." Shortly before the end of the war the Minneapolis *Star Tribune* in its lead editorial stated: "First in the skies of Kuwait and Iraq, now in their sands, the United States is finding military redemption."[2]

U.S. leaders, from their perspective, had carried out a near perfect war. The war was swift, decisive, and, through the lens of press bias and censorship, efficient. Equally important they had fashioned the most compelling moral justification for war: good versus evil. Saddam Hussein was equated with Hitler: demonic, insane, brutal, and poised to threaten not only his immediate neighbors but Western Civilization, indeed the whole world. "Most Americans know instinctively why we are in the Gulf," President Bush told the nation. "They know we had to stop Saddam now, not later. They know that this brutal dictator will do anything, will use any weapon, will commit any outrage, no matter how many innocents suffer." "Tonight," he said, "we work to achieve another victory, a victory over tyranny and savage aggression."[3] In the context of widespread patriotic fever few people asked why the United States had suddenly transformed Saddam Hussein from a U.S.-supported regional power broker into a global menace.

Saddam Hussein personified an unspeakable evil, which demanded its opposite. Only the United States, the prevailing view maintained, could provide the necessary moral leadership and military force. "America has both the moral standing and the means to back it up," President Bush said during his State of the Union Address. "We're the only nation on this Earth that could assemble the forces of peace." U.S. soldiers were portrayed as the arm of God fighting a war reminiscent of the crusades.

The promised fruits of victory were as wondrous as the enemy was evil. The United States, with God on our side, would use its military might both to liberate Kuwait and to fashion a "new world order." "What is at stake is more than one small country," President Bush stated. "It is a big idea: a new world order, where diverse nations are drawn together in common cause to achieve the universal aspirations of mankind—peace and security, freedom, and the rule of law."

This new world order is being founded on an updated version of manifest destiny. It is the "moral duty" of the United States to expand greatly its use of military force. "Kicking butt," a euphemistic phrase commonly used to describe U.S. policy in the Gulf, is not only morally defensible in trouble spots throughout an unruly world; it is a requirement of morality itself. "We are Americans; we have a unique responsibility to do the hard work of freedom," President Bush proclaimed. "The conviction and courage we see in the Persian Gulf today is simply the American character in action."

## Contradictions

I was in Central America when the U.S.-led military offensive against Iraq began. Central America is in shambles after more than a decade of U.S.-sponsored warfare. As a direct consequence of U.S. policy, countries in the region see their economies crumbling, their living standards eroding, and infant mortality and malnutrition on the rise. Earlier experiences in Central America led me to write a book highly critical of U.S. policy, *War Against the Poor: Low-Intensity Conflict and Christian Faith*. It also led me to be deeply suspicious of U.S. objectives in the Gulf and of U.S. pretensions about a new world order.

President Bush spoke eloquently about U.S. objectives in his State of the Union Address of January 29, 1991:

> We will succeed in the Gulf. And when we do, the world community will have sent an enduring warning to any dictator or despot, present or future, who contemplates outlaw aggression. The world can, therefore, seize this opportunity to fulfill the long-held promise of a new world order, where brutality will go unrewarded and aggression will meet collective resistance. . . . The cost of closing our eyes to aggression is beyond mankind's power to imagine. This we do know: Our cause is just; our cause is moral; our cause is right.

As I listened to these words I couldn't help but remember other, more compelling words, written to President Bush in a letter from the Latin American Council of Churches in the aftermath of the murders of the Jesuit priests by U.S.-backed forces in El Salvador:

> How long? How long will the Christians and people of the United States have to contemplate the incongruity of its government . . . as it supports with over a million dollars a day another government that represses, kills bishops, religious workers, children, men and women, violates human rights, closes itself to dialogue and obstructs the pastoral task of the churches? . . . How long? In the name of the God of Justice, in the name of Jesus Christ, Prince of Peace, in the name of the Spirit of all truth: stop now.[4]

The rhetoric surrounding U.S. objectives in the Gulf was contradicted by actual policy in Central America. For example, less than two weeks before his State of the Union Address, and on the same day he authorized U.S. military force in the Gulf, President Bush announced his intention to release $42.5 million in military aid to the government of El Salvador. He did so even though no progress had been made in prosecuting the Jesuit murders, a key condition of aid. There were other contradictions:

• U.S. leaders said we were fighting in the Gulf so that big countries would be deterred from aggression against little countries, yet the United States had itself invaded Panama and Grenada, had waged a bloody war against Nicaragua, and continued major involvement in El Salvador's civil war.

• President Bush called Saddam Hussein's invasion of Kuwait "an assault on the very notion of international law,"[5] and U.S. leaders repeatedly cited commitment to international law to justify their actions, yet the United States had withdrawn from the World Court and failed to heed World Court decisions requiring it to cease its illegal war against Nicaragua and to pay billions of dollars in reparations.

• U.S. leaders used Saddam Hussein's failure to heed United Nations' resolutions as a principal justification for the use of military force against Iraq. For example, President Bush, in a radio address to the nation on January 5, said that "eleven days from today, Saddam Hussein will either have met the United Nations deadline for a full and unconditional withdrawal or he will have once again defied the civilized world."[6] However, the United States has consistently ignored or undermined U.N. resolutions that challenge U.S. misconduct or that of its allies. The United States ignored U.N. resolutions condemning its invasions of Panama and Grenada, and its bombing of Libya in retaliation for a terrorist attack in Germany that was later linked to Syria, a new U.S. ally. It also cast the lone no vote against a U.N. resolution, approved by a vote of 156 to 1, calling for an end to the arms race in space, and continued to support Israel despite that country's illegal occupation of Palestine, which the United Nations had condemned on more than seventy occasions.

• U.S. leaders said that Saddam Hussein was a threat to our way of life, yet the vast majority of people in Central America, and throughout much of the Third World, experience poverty and oppression as a direct result of U.S. military and economic intervention.

• Ironically, President Bush, who rewarded the murderers of the Jesuit priests in El Salvador, repeatedly cited human rights issues to garner support for U.S. policy in the Gulf. He nearly wept in a January 2 interview with David Frost as he discussed an Amnesty International report describing violations of human rights by Iraqi forces against Kuwaiti citizens:

> *Frost:* What particularly struck you in that Amnesty report?
>
> *President Bush:* Oh, David, it was so terrible, it's hard to describe. Just to give you a little background on this, I handed it to Barbara as we left Camp David. And she read about two pages of it and said, "I can't read anymore." But the torturing of a handicapped child. The shooting of young boys in front of their parents. The rape of women dragged out of the home and repeatedly raped and then brought to the hospital as kind of basket cases. The tying of those that are being tortured to ceiling fans so they turn and turn. . . . Electric shots to the private—shocks to the private parts of men and women. Broken glass inserted in—jabbed into people. I mean, it—it is primeval. And I— I'm afraid I'd get very emotional if I described—described more of it. The hitting on they call it—falanga or something like that—hitting on the bottom of the feet so a 15-year-old kid can't walk. The passing out of leaflets and then, for that, you are tortured so you can't even talk or move. It is outrageous what's happened.
>
> *Frost:* It's sort of—genocide in a way, isn't it?
>
> *President Bush:* Well, it is. It's a deliberate wiping them out.[7]

President Bush apparently chose to ignore numerous other reports from Amnesty International, including at least three which didn't serve his foreign policy objectives: "Saudi Arabia: Detention without Trial of Suspected Political Prisoners," January 1990; "Saudi Arabia: Torture, Detention, and Arbitrary Arrests," October 1990; and "El Salvador: Killings, Torture and Disappearances," October 1990. In short, there are ample historical reasons that justify caution or suspicion in relation to U.S. policy goals in the Gulf and its objectives within the so-called new world order. Unfortunately, as *Brave New World Order* makes clear, the problem is not that the United States is pursuing moral policies in the Gulf and immoral policies in Central America. Its foreign policy is remarkably consistent. The challenge undertaken in *Brave New World Order* is to expose the intent and strategy of the Gulf War and its utility for U.S. leaders as they fashion this new world order.

I have obviously chosen the title *Brave New World Order* in reference to Aldous Huxley's novel *Brave New World*. Huxley's novel depicts a utopian world where order has been achieved at the expense of compassion, human freedom, and creativity. John, a principle character in the novel, is eager to embrace a new world he has yet to see. This new world ends up tormenting him, and he eventually ends his nightmare by taking his own life. *Brave New World* is a chilling reminder that utopian rhetoric must always be carefully scrutinized. Because an authentically new world order is a real need in our time, we, like John, may be too eager to embrace it without first having seen or experienced it. By naming this book *Brave New World Order* I am stating my grave concern about harmful U.S. policies that are disguised through alluring rhetoric as a "new world order."

*Brave New World Order* seeks to unmask the veneer of moral purpose surrounding the U.S.-led war in the Middle East and the new world order it reflects and ushers in. It seeks to expose the dangerous idolatry and hypocrisy of church and state. It calls for an authentically new world order involving a radical transformation of national and international priorities, which must begin with a radical transformation of the church itself.

Chapter 1, "Brave New Third-World Order," explores the relationship between Western economies and the forty million human beings who die each year from hunger or hunger-related causes. This is a new world order designed by the rich to consolidate their power at the expense of the poor. This chapter describes the mechanisms used in the "new" order by the United States, including the economic policing function of the International Monetary Fund (IMF), to ensure continued economic domination of third-world countries.

Chapter 2, "Brave New First-World Order," examines the new world order in light of U.S. poverty and economic decline. It explores the policy options confronting the United States in the post–Cold War period in which it is the weakest economic link in a tripolar world dominated by Japan and Western

Europe. It describes the factors contributing to U.S. social and economic decay and the particular economic and military interests that are served by the Gulf War and which dominate the "new" order.

Chapter 3, "National Security State Doctrine and the New World Order," outlines dangerous features of a National Security State, with specific illustrations from El Salvador. It demonstrates how the institutional imperatives of the Salvadoran military have undermined Salvadoran democracy and prospects for peace. This chapter lays a foundation for Chapter 4, "The U.S. National Security State," which explores the evolution and power of the U.S. National Security Establishment. It is this group that is most threatened by the prospect of a peace dividend, most resistant to economic revitalization, and most committed to a new world order based on U.S. military supremacy.

Chapter 5, "Policing the Brave New World Order," explores the role of the United States within a changing world order in which North-South conflicts are intensifying as East-West hostilities diminish. It documents the situation of near panic with which the U.S. military and related complex greeted the end of the Cold War, their search for new enemies, and their plans for institutional survival at the expense of the U.S. economy and third-world peoples.

Chapter 6, "The Gulf War and the Brave New World Order," documents how the U.S. National Security Establishment created and exploited the crisis in the Middle East. The Gulf War was a premeditated and highly successful effort to foreclose on the peace dividend and to create a new world order in which U.S. superpower status is guaranteed on the basis of military power rather than economic health. The intentional militarization of the Gulf crisis provides further evidence that U.S. democracy has been seriously compromised by the prerogatives of a National Security State.

Chapter 7, "Environmental Disorder in the Brave New World Order," probes whether the new order is capable of saving the planet. The two most pressing issues facing humanity as we approach and enter the twenty-first century are overcoming the oppression of the poor and the transition to sustainable societies. These two monumental tasks are deeply interrelated. The

Worldwatch Institute warns that we have approximately forty years to make the transition to a sustainable future. This transition involves a dramatic change in values, technology and patterns of production and consumption. It also depends on radically improving the living standards of the poor.[8] Unfortunately, the new world order with its emphasis on militarism, consumerism, debt-induced austerity, and development at the expense of oppressed peoples and overburdened ecosystems will likely accelerate the earth's destruction.

Chapter 8, "Mark, Jesus, and the Kingdom: Confronting World Orders, Old and New," examines Jesus' confrontation with the world order of his day. It explores the relevancy of this confrontation for those of us who seek to unmask the "brave new world order" of U.S. leaders and who seek an authentic new order more reflective of kingdom values.

Chapter 9, "The Church, the Gulf War, and the New World Order," outlines the theological significance of religious complicity with the new world order. The most compelling analogy between the recent war in the Middle East and Nazi Germany is the blind patriotism that infected the German people and churches and the idolatrous patriotism sweeping through our country and our churches. The new world order envisioned by U.S. leaders dramatically clashes with the values and priorities of Jesus and the kingdom. Religious complicity with such an order points to a dramatic faith crisis in which idolatry undermines the integrity of faith.

We are living in a decisive moment in history. Our faithful response to the new world order requires us to break radically from the dominating culture. We cannot claim to be followers of Jesus unless overcoming oppression and insuring the survival of the earth are central issues in our lives. These priorities clash sharply with the brave new world order envisioned by U.S. leaders and embraced by many people of faith. *Brave New World Order* not only condemns the injustice of the so-called new order; it lifts up the possibility of an authentic new world order more reflective of Jesus' vision and values. It offers suggestions on how people of faith, joining together in small communities, can creatively withdraw from, confront, and transform our society, beginning with our churches.

## CHAPTER 1

# Brave New Third-World Order

*We also predestine and condition. We decant our babies as
socialized human beings . . . as future sewage workers or future
. . . He was going to say "future World controllers," but cor-
recting himself, said "future Directors of Hatcheries."*
> —A worker in *Brave New World's*
> Social Predestination Room

*But someone is always going to have to lead the civilized
world.*
> —Michael Kramer, "Read My Ships," *Time*,
> August 20, 1990

The brave new world order being fashioned by the United
States is based on clearly defined roles. U.S. leaders are "pre-
destined" to be world controllers. Poor people in and outside
of the United States are being "conditioned" to accept their
place as the equivalent of "future sewage workers" in Aldous
Huxley's novel. President Bush has suggested that in the new
world order the weak must learn to trust the mercy of the strong.
Unfortunately, as we will see, the weak can expect neither mercy
nor justice in the new order.

The new world order is not fixed in time. It is an ongoing
process of realignment among the powerful with profound implications for rich and poor both within the United States and the
so-called Third World. The phrase itself, *new world order*, is

misleading. If you replace your twenty-year-old jalopy with a new car or move from a rundown, cockroach-infested apartment to a new house in a comfortable neighborhood, then it is appropriate to think of your situation as new. If on the other hand you put new tires on your old car and fumigate your old apartment, then you are adapting to your situation. In the first case the changes are fundamental. They mark a dramatic rupture with the past. In the latter case the situation has changed in important but less dramatic ways; there is clear continuity with the past.

One important feature of the new world order is that it isn't really new. Joel Beinin, Professor of Middle Eastern History at Stanford University, notes:

> The Bush Administration's response to this [Middle East] crisis is an indication of its strategy to maintain a leading American role in the post–Cold War world. Bush has spoken of this as a "new world order." But in fact it is the same old stuff ... American intervention in the Third World to secure access to resources and markets and maintain the political status quo.[1]

The *new world order* is a new phase in an ongoing history of U.S. control over third-world peoples and resources. The "same old stuff" is also evident in a "new" order in which U.S. policy emphasizes military solutions. "On the road to failure," Beinin says, this policy "will mark a very high economic cost on this country.... The resources that will be expended on the military will be resources that cannot be but should have been spent on our own people here at home."[2]

The new order, like the old, is concerned with the relative distribution of wealth and power. The old order's most powerful players are struggling to adapt to changing circumstances. These circumstances include the decline of the Soviet Union, reduced East-West tensions, growing conflict between the developed nations of the North and the underdeveloped nations of the South, unrestrained U.S. military power, regional conflicts in the Third World, and economic realignment among Western nations, including the economic decline of the United States. In addition to the obvious shift in the balance of military power in the post-Cold War period there are three major economic trends that are shaking the foundations of the old order. Each involves a massive transfer of wealth:

- from poor nations to rich nations;
- from U.S. poor and working-class people, and from future generations, to U.S elites; and,
- from the United States to Japan and Western Europe.

Shifts in the balance of military and economic power, which confront U.S. leaders with numerous problems and contradictions, hold the key to unmasking the motivation of U.S. leaders during the Gulf War and to understanding the broader policy objectives of the United States within the new world order. Maintaining the skewed concentration of wealth within the United States while continuing to transfer wealth from the third-world poor to the developed-country rich are key objectives of the new world order. However, these trends, deliberate and interrelated, are based on systematic exploitation. They are likely to foment considerable unrest both domestically and internationally. The economic decline of the United States relative to its Western allies poses other serious problems for a country that wants to exercise undisputed leadership in a new world order. U.S. economic problems are aggravated by the conflict between economic revitalization and a new world order in which the United States is assuming, in the words of the London *Financial Times*, a more "mercenary role."[3] President Bush and other U.S. leaders are adapting to and shaping a world order that suits *particular* interests. This chapter examines mechanisms within the new order whereby the third-world poor continue to subsidize the first-world rich.

## A Third-World Perspective on Who "Won" the Cold War

The nonviolent movements that swept through Eastern Europe and the rapid fall of the Soviet Union from superpower status surprised the world, but the process of disintegration had deep historical roots. Nonetheless, bureaucratic communist parties and the command economies they directed seemed to be discredited overnight. Unfortunately, in the West the interpretation of these events was generally limited to self-congratulation rather than self-criticism. The Cold War was over, and we had won; *we,* of course, referred to the United States, the West, and capitalism. Democracy and the international market system had triumphed.

"Winning" the Cold War, for the United States, is an ideological triumph rooted in lies, distortions, and historical blindness. It is possible to proclaim victory because the failures of the Soviet-dominated order are real and obvious and because important facts are suppressed. For example, one of four U.S. children is born into poverty.[4] This statistic symbolically illustrates a deeper crisis: as the Cold War ended the United States was the lone global military superpower but was the weakest economic partner in a tripolar world dominated by Japan and Western Europe. The dynamics of this crisis, and its relation to the new world order, are the subject of Chapter 2.

If claims of victory in the Cold War are dubious in light of childhood poverty and U.S. economic decline, then they are also questionable from the perspective of third-world peoples whose countries are allied with the "victorious" Western powers. Pablo Richard, a liberation theologian working in Costa Rica, writes:

> The world changed abruptly in the last months of 1989. . . . But has the life and death situation of the poor and oppressed masses of the Third World really changed? The Berlin Wall fell, and the rich world trembled with joy. In reality, the fall of the wall was very positive. But we are aware that another gigantic wall is being constructed in the Third World, to hide the reality of the poor majorities. A wall between the rich and the poor is being built, so that poverty does not annoy the powerful and the poor are obliged to die in the silence of history. A wall of silence is being built so that the rich world forgets the Third World. A wall of disinformation . . . is being built to casually pervert the reality of the Third World.[5]

In addition to the reality of childhood poverty within the "victorious" United States is the fact that the majority of the approximately forty million people who die each year from hunger live in third-world nations dominated by the United States and its Western allies. The victims of hunger and poverty are not primarily casualties of the Soviet Empire. They are victims of the international market economy which is being heralded as the savior of Eastern Europe and all of humanity.[6]

The uncritical patriotism that swept through the United States following the war against Iraq was built on the earlier sense of triumph in the Cold War. U.S. claims of victory in the Cold War, of moral legitimacy in the Gulf War, and of moral purpose in the new world order are rooted in national self-deception. Such deception, including the use of the collective "we" in the proclamation of victory, is highly misleading and dangerous: it hides the ongoing oppression of the poor, within and outside the United States; it conceals the economic decline of the United States relative to Western Europe and Japan; and, it obscures fundamental contradictions and conflicts within U.S. domestic and foreign policies that benefit certain groups at the expense of others.

### Third-World Coverup

Jon Sobrino, a Jesuit priest from El Salvador, speaks of the self-deception of the First World or Western countries as a scandalous coverup. Shortly after the murder of two women and six priests at the hands of U.S.-trained soldiers in El Salvador he wrote:

> Wealth and power cannot exist if other people do not die, if people do not suffer in powerlessness and poverty and without dignity.... We say that the First World, the wealthy countries, cover up the greatest scandal in this world, which is the world itself. The existence of two-thirds of humankind dying in poverty is covered up.[7]

The poor majorities living in Latin America, the Caribbean, the Philippines, and many other third-world countries find little comfort in hearing that the Cold War is over and "we" won. Their countries have been integrated into the international market economy for generations, and they are living in nations with close political, economic, and military ties to the United States. Presumably, they are on the winning side of the Cold War conflict. However, their lives are condemned to poverty, inequality, and oppression.

The contradiction should be obvious. We rightly equate food shortages and long lines in the Soviet Union with the failures of communism, but we fail to see domestic and international hunger in light of the failure of capitalism and the international market economy. The United States celebrates democratic movements and social changes in Eastern Europe. However, it blocks the possibility of similar changes within the U.S. sphere of influence. *Processo*, a journal of the Catholic University (UCA) in San Salvador, implicitly highlights U.S. hypocrisy by contrasting the fate of opposition leaders in Eastern Europe with that of leaders in U.S.-dominated El Salvador:

> The so-called Salvadoran "democratic process" could learn a lot from the capacity for self-criticism that the socialist nations are demonstrating. If Lech Walesa had been doing his organizing work in El Salvador, he would have already entered into the ranks of the disappeared — at the hands of "heavily armed men dressed in civilian clothes"; or have been blown to pieces in a dynamite attack on his union headquarters. If Alexander Dubcek were a politician in our country, he would have been assassinated like Hector Oqueli [a social democratic leader killed by Salvadoran death squads in Guatemala]. If Andrei Sakharov had worked here in favor of human rights, he would have met the same fate as Herbert Anaya [assassinated leader of the Non-governmental Human Rights Commission]. If Ota-Sik or Vaclav Havel had been carrying out their intellectual work in El Salvador, they would have woken up one sinister morning, lying on the patio of a university campus with their heads destroyed by the bullets of an elite army battalion.[8]

The poor desperately need a new world order. However, an authentically new order would require a fundamental break with the old. Not only was victory in the Cold War an empty claim for underdeveloped countries but the new world order that is taking shape in the post–Cold War period is solidifying an alliance of Northern industrialized countries against the nations of the South.

## Wealth Transfers and Third-World Poverty

The new world order is ruled primarily by two global police forces: a military force dominated by the United States (see Chapters 5 and 6), and an economic force controlled by the United States and other Western powers. The "global economic cop" is the International Monetary Fund (IMF), which works closely with private Western banks and the World Bank to guide the international economy in preferred directions. Neither of these "global cops" is new, but their power has grown considerably within the framework of a new world order. Together they ensure a continuous transfer of wealth from the poor to the rich.

The poor can rightfully protest police brutality at the hands of these "global cops" and their allies within third-world countries. The poor are victims of structural violence and injustice within the old order and the new. They are victimized not once, but twice. First, they are casualties of injustice within their own nations, because most third-world leaders organize economic and human resources to enhance the power and privilege of internal elites. Second, they are victims of injustice within the global economy, which is structured by Western countries to drain wealth from underdeveloped countries to themselves. This amounts to a double dose of exploitation for the third-world poor. They are marginalized within their own societies, and they are impoverished by an unjust international order that serves the needs of external elites.

There are often tensions between internal and external elites. Each group seeks to enhance its relative position within a highly unequal yet mutually beneficial global order. These tensions can be profound because Western powers often treat third-world elites as junior partners. However, the well-being of each group ultimately depends on cooperation. Also, the two global police forces are vigilant. If third-world elites get out of line, or for one reason or another lose power, the United States and other Western nations can use sophisticated forms of economic and military intervention to restore order.[9] The important point for this discussion is that both national and international elites pursue their interests at the expense of the poor.

The poor are excluded from meaningful participation in economic life in most third-world countries. According to the World Bank, it is common for two or three percent of the landholders to control seventy to eighty percent of the land.[10] Banks are owned or controlled by foreigners, rich business owners, the state, or military officials, who are becoming major economic actors in some societies. Commercial banks rarely if ever make loans to poor people, who are by definition not credit worthy. If small landowners get credit from a bank, they risk losing their land, which they use as collateral. From biblical times to the present foreclosing on debt has been an important means of transferring land from the poor to the rich. Generally speaking, poor people live without credit or live in bondage to usurious moneylenders.

Industrial and agricultural production throughout much of the Third World caters to export markets and elite consumption. These sectors are highly concentrated and subject to significant foreign influence and control. Jobs in the commercial sector, when available to the poor, are limited to seasonal agricultural work and unskilled factory work. It is not uncommon for poor majorities to be unemployed or underemployed. The subsistence agricultural sector and local craft industries, so important to the poor, are ignored and/or often undermined by official development efforts. The problems of the poor are compounded by corruption, political repression, and terror. Independent labor unions and other social change groups are treated harshly.

The victimization of the poor within unjust internal orders is not limited to their exclusion from meaningful participation in the economic life of their societies. They also bear the brunt of budget cuts, are often excluded from social services, and are ignored when their societies invest in human capital.

The rich live in exclusive neighborhoods with nice houses, running water, sewer lines, schools, hospitals, clinics, and parks. They gain access to good health care, education, and nutrition through a combination of private wealth and political power. Their money makes health care, housing, and food affordable. It also gives them a privileged place in politics. Political influence then allows them to shape public policies that reinforce their wealth-producing endeavors. It also enables them to direct limited public funding to meet their needs for schools, hospitals, clinics, and the basic infrastructure such as roads, sewers, and water.

The situation of the poor is just the opposite. The poor live in shanty towns and shacks. Running water is the stream of raw sewage winding among their homes. Their houses, often found at the bottom of ravines, are a collage of tin, plastic, cardboard and wood. In urban areas one or two water taps may be the only water source for hundreds of families — and water may flow from these taps for only a couple of hours each day. In rural areas women and children often spend a significant part of each day gathering water and firewood from distant sources.

The poor, in stark contrast to the rich, are denied access to housing, health care, education, and adequate nutrition. They have little economic power and even less political clout. The poor lack political power, and therefore they are unable to shape public policies to redistribute wealth-producing resources or to fund education, health care, potable water, sewers, housing, and roads that will meet their needs.

The typical job of the poor is to survive. The fact that many do survive is a major testimony to the creativity and resiliency of the poor. That many do not is part of a coverup that is central to world orders both old and new.

The unbearable situation of the poor under oppressive national orders is reinforced by an unjust international order. President Bush's new world order is coming on the heels of a decade that witnessed the largest transfer of wealth from the third-world poor to the developed-country rich in human history. The recent massive drain of wealth from the South to the North is reminiscent of the colonial conquest. In 1989 alone, third-world peoples sent $52 billion more in debt payments to developed countries in the North than their nations received in new credits.[11]

The third-world poor blatantly subsidize the developed-country rich because the two global police forces do their jobs effectively. The United States reinforces a global economy based on unfair trade practices and exploits third-world indebtedness through a combination of military and economic intervention. Third-world countries for decades have demanded fairer terms of trade within a new international economic order. The response of Western countries, with leadership from the United States, has been to defend a system dominated by unfair pricing while offering loans to financially strapped third-world countries. Today, loans to underdeveloped countries are either drying up or are highly conditional. If a third-world country wants access to loans from international lending institutions and private banks, then it must agree to specific terms that often result in greater exploitation.

The United States, when it suits its interests, believes in free trade and in the utility of letting market forces set international prices. The discrediting of command economies rightfully reinforces a belief that markets have an important role to play within national economies and international trade. Michael Harrington, perhaps the best-known U.S. socialist, wrote before the upheaval in Eastern Europe that "markets have an important role to play in the new socialism."[12] However, free trade is rarely free. For example, about eighty percent of textile and apparel imports into the United States are restrained by thirty-four quota agreements, mostly with developing countries, and there are about 160 "voluntary" export restraints in place to prevent the free movement of goods into the United States and Europe.[13]

Free trade may be fine among equal partners. However, it is a prescription for disaster in a world of stark inequalities. Unjust terms of trade coupled with loans to the Third World have resulted in a $1.3 trillion debt among the world's underdeveloped countries. Exploitation of this debt is now a major means of transferring wealth from the poor to the rich.

One problem with free trade is that the international market economy is dominated by multinational corporations and banks. These groups, which pursue and defend specific interests, are directly and indirectly responsible for the misery and deaths of millions of third-world people. Most underdeveloped countries depend on revenues from a few export commodities to finance development. These commodities, according to the Ecumenical Coalition for Economic Justice, are often "sold on world markets where prices are set in U.S. dollars under conditions of very imperfect competition." Markets for most primary commodities are "dominated by a few corporations." Poor countries are selling their commodities in "markets where many sellers face only a few powerful buyers."[14]

The United Nations Commission on Trade and Development (UNCTAD) estimates that three to six corporations control a high percentage of trade in the following commodities:

| | |
|---|---|
| sugar | 60% |
| bananas | 70-75% |
| crude oil | 75% |
| tin | 75-80% |
| tea | 80% |
| copper and bauxite | 80-85% |
| wheat, coffee, cocoa, cotton, and jute | 85-90% |
| pineapples and forest products | 90% |
| iron ore | 90-95%[15] |

A large number of sellers selling to a few number of buyers is a characteristic of a free-market system in which weaker parties in the "free" transaction lose out. Depressed commodity prices are common to such an unequal free market. Falling commodity prices are a major factor in the economic crisis plaguing underdeveloped countries and they directly and indirectly contribute to hunger and starvation. Between 1986 and 1988 sub-Saharan Africa lost $50 billion in export earnings due to lower commodity prices.[16]

The Western strategy of providing limited aid to compensate partially for an unfair trading system is by most accounts a gross failure. Aid, often self-serving and highly conditional, doesn't compensate for lost income from unfair trading practices and capital transfers to the rich through rising debt payments and capital flight. Eighty percent of the cash flow between the rich and poor nations occurs through trade, only five percent through aid. In 1985 emergency aid from all sources to Africa was approximately $3 billion. That same year Africa paid $6 billion in interest payments and lost an additional $19 billion in export earnings due to price collapses on the international market.[17]

The poor may not directly benefit from higher commodity prices because wealth-producing resources are concentrated in the hands of internal elites. However, they are most directly victimized by burdensome debts that are aggravated by low commodity prices and low export earnings. Low commodity prices lead to third-world country debt. Debt for the poor leads to suffering and oftentimes death.

Death through international finance is a central feature of world orders old and new. Indebtedness gives the IMF substantial policing power over third-world nations. The IMF, as the economic enforcer in the new world order, uses its power on behalf of the United States and other developed countries to achieve three important objectives. First, IMF policies ensure a continuous transfer of wealth to rich countries through interest payments on third-world country debt. Second, the IMF imposes conditions on third-world economies that result in their continued integration into an unjust international order. Finally, IMF policies encourage greater foreign penetration and control of the resources and economies of indebted third-world countries.

The principal tools in the IMF arsenal are austerity measures imposed through structural adjustment programs (SAPs). The Ecumenical Coalition for Economic Justice describes the impact of these SAPs on third-world countries:

> Instead of developing their own resources to meet pressing human needs, many Third World economies are literally being "sapped" — gradually exhausted of their wealth — through conditions imposed by their creditors. The goals of this new colonialism are, in part, the same as the old. Thanks to SAPs, transnational corporations enjoy greater access to cheap raw materials, cheap labour and foreign markets. But ... the contemporary recolonization also involves an annual collection of tribute in the form of interest payments on debts that ... can never be paid off.

Thanks to the "success" of SAPs, debt bondage is becoming permanent.[18]

Phrases such as the "new colonialism" and "contemporary recolonization" are synonyms for the new world order in which the IMF plays the role of global economic cop.

The standard features of the structural adjustment programs imposed by the IMF and the World Bank include currency devaluations; higher interest rates; strict control of the money supply; cuts in government spending; removal of trade and exchange controls; the use of market forces to set the prices of goods, services, and labor; privatization of public sector enterprises; and indiscriminate export promotion. These measures, according to IMF theory, should result in lower inflation, increased exports, reduced consumption and imports, greater efficiency, international competitiveness, and substantial foreign exchange earnings available for debt repayments.

SAPs in practice have been a dramatic success for first-world elites and a dramatic failure for the third-world poor. Between 1982 and 1989 the net outflow of debt service from underdeveloped countries to the developed countries, that is, the amount of capital exported in excess of new loans, equalled $240 billion.[19] Despite this massive transfer of wealth from the poor to the rich the World Bank reports that in the five years after 1982 no country rescheduling its debts actually reduced the ratio of that debt to its gross national product.[20]

The problem of third-world indebtedness worsened considerably because of decisions made by U.S. elites, which sent U.S. indebtedness and global interest rates soaring. Unfortunately, "sewage workers" pay when "world controllers" make "mistakes."

Between 1978 and 1983 Latin America's total interest payments increased by 360 per cent. By 1984 every 1 per cent rise in interest rates was in effect adding $700 million to the annual payments of Brazil alone. By 1990 Latin America's debts were four times as large as its total annual earnings from exports which meant that every 1 per cent rise in interest rates necessitated a 4 per cent increase in exports if the continent was to pay.[21]

Growing indebtedness means greater vulnerability to IMF-prescribed "solutions." There are at least seven ways in which the SAPs imposed by the IMF and World Bank negatively effect underdeveloped countries and poor people within them. First, *an emphasis on production for export, a standard feature of SAPs, further weakens the subsistence sector while strengthening the sectors dominated by foreigners.* These export sectors tend to rely upon *imported* raw materials and technology. The cost of such imports can actually aggravate the debt crisis. More important, the commercial export sector's reliance on foreign inputs and foreign markets precludes the possibility of strengthening a domestic economy in which agriculture serves local needs, including food production for local consumption and production of raw materials for use in a domestically oriented commercial sector. The agricultural sector is reduced to an export factory that feeds the insatiable appetite of the debt and not people. Thus SAPs become a prescription for hunger, malnutrition, and environmental deterioration. "Development" within the framework of SAPs is limited to an IMF plan for export-led debt repayment.

A second negative consequence of SAPs is that the *emphasis on exports can result in overproduction and a further deterioration in the terms of trade.* The Ecumenical Coalition for Economic Justice describes how this happens, who benefits, and who loses:

> While it might appear to make sense for a single country to try to improve its export earnings by increasing the volume of its sales, when thirty countries that export the same basic products try to do so, they end up driving down prices. The only winners are the corporate buyers. As commodity prices fall, already exploited peasant farmers, miners and workers are told they have to take price or wage cuts to remain competitive, further subsidizing corporate profits.[22]

Third, the *higher interest rates mandated by SAPs often encourage speculation, fuel inflation, and further aggravate class divisions*

*by limiting lending to the most affluent and powerful economic
sectors.* Higher interest rates may also discourage productive
investment and thereby further depress ailing economies, aggra-
vating already serious problems of unemployment.

Fourth, *removal of trade and export controls fosters dependence
on foreign inputs, increases the domination of foreign firms over
third-world economies, and encourages capital flight.* "A good portion of the money lent to the Third World and in particular to
Latin American countries has mysteriously found its way back
to U.S. banks," writes journalist Paul Vallely, "but in the personal accounts of influential Latin Americans." Elites from
Latin America and the Caribbean have more than $200 billion
worth of assets in the United States.[23] Capital flight is another
example of how the third-world poor subsidize the first-world
rich. Elites exploit the poor and then transfer their wealth to
U.S. and other Western banks.

Fifth, *privatization encouraged by SAPs can result in greater
concentrations of wealth and a loss of economic sovereignty.* Privatization offers local elites and foreign investors the opportunity to purchase publicly developed enterprises at sharply
discounted prices. It is particularly profitable when linked to
debt equity swaps. Debt equity swaps are a means by which
foreign investors use debt as leverage to take over important
sectors of third-world country economies. A commercial bank
in a debt equity transaction sells a portion of the debt owed to
it by a third-world country to a corporation at a discount. The
corporation receives from the country's central bank the value
of the debt purchased in local currency, which is then invested
as equity in local enterprises.

Sixth, *mandated currency devaluations erode the purchasing
power of workers while benefiting foreign corporations operating in
export zones.* For example, as a result of devaluations of the
Mexican peso the U.S. dollar cost of employing young women
in Mexico's export processing zones fell by two-thirds.[24]

Finally, *in order to satisfy foreign creditors third-world governments drastically reduce government spending.* Spending cuts can
undermine future development by reducing funds for economic
and social infrastructure. They also aggravate problems of hunger and poverty. One reason third-world elites cooperate with

the IMF is because they place the weight of painful adjustments on the backs of the poor. SAPs lead to dramatic spending reductions in areas of food subsidies, health, and education. According to the United Nations children's organization (UNICEF) the world's thirty-seven poorest countries cut health-care budgets by fifty percent and education budgets by twenty-five percent in the 1980s. UNICEF estimates that more than a million African children died in the last decade as a result of structural adjustment programs imposed on the poor. In 1988 alone, according to UNICEF, 500,000 children died in underdeveloped countries as a direct result of SAP-induced austerity measures. UNICEF has concluded:

> It is essential to strip away the niceties of economic parlance and say that . . . the developing world's debt, both in the manner in which it was incurred and in the manner in which it is being "adjusted to" . . . is simply an outrage against a large section of humanity.[25]

Third-world elites also cooperate with the IMF because their power is tied to foreign economic interests. "The third world elites who borrowed the money," Jorge Sol, a former IMF executive director for Central America, states, ". . . come from the same class as those who lent it and as those who managed it at the IMF. They went to the same schools, belonged to the same clubs. They all profited greatly from the debt. They will not turn on those interests."[26]

SAPs are a disaster for the poor, and they fail to achieve officially stated goals. However, from the perspective of first-world elites, the International Monetary Fund and its partner, the World Bank, police the world order with great efficiency. The Ecumenical Coalition for Economic Justice provides the following summary:

> Given the evidence that SAPs do not achieve their official goals, that they cause immense hunger and misery and they accentuate underdevelopment, why do private bankers, the IMF, the World Bank and conservative governments insist on their strict application? . . . Viewed from the perspec-

tive of transnational investors, SAPs do make sense. SAPs assure transnational corporations that countries on the periphery will supply abundant supplies of cheap raw materials, low-wage labour and markets for some of their products. SAPs enable transnationals to maintain control over manufacturing processes, technology and finance, sharing some of the spoils with local elites. In addition, SAPs promote exports that earn foreign exchange to service otherwise unpayable debts.[27]

## Conclusion

Jon Sobrino's charge that wealthy countries "cover up the greatest scandal in this world, which is the world itself" is more comprehensible in light of the above analysis. The new world order is being structured on the backs of the poor and on behalf of transnational corporations and banks. The poor are discovering that the end of the Cold War leaves them even more vulnerable to a new world order in which the North is increasingly united against the South. One major objective of this new order is to ensure the continued integration of third-world economies into an inherently unjust system. Two global police forces ensure this integration, the most important of which is the International Monetary Fund. The other is the U.S. military, which justifies itself in the post–Cold War period on the basis of third-world interventionism (see chapter 6) but which may in fact be less important because of effective control achieved through institutions such as the IMF.

The structural roots of massive third-world poverty testify to the need for a radical break with both old and new orders of the dominant powers. An authentically new world order would condemn both the command economies dominated by elite bureaucratic parties and the international market economy dominated by national and international elites. It would also dismantle the economic policing powers of the International Monetary Fund.

The circle of victims of the new order extends well beyond the Third World. It includes the majority of U.S. citizens. It is to this topic that we now turn.

## CHAPTER 2

# Brave New First-World Order

---

*The forces of the late twentieth century have required double-entry bookkeeping: new wealth in profusion for the bright, the bold, the educated and the politically favored; economic carnage among the less fortunate. In short, the United States of the 1980s.*

— Kevin Phillips, *The Politics of Rich and Poor*

Poor people living in third-world countries are not the only victims of the so-called new world order. At the heart of this "new" order is a troubling paradox: *Poor people within the United States, and the country as a whole, are getting poorer at the same time as the rich within the United States are getting richer*. The massive wealth drain from third-world countries to first-world elites has not prevented the economic decline of the United States. Its pressing national problems mirror those of many third-world countries. The infant mortality rate in inner cities like Detroit and Washington, D.C., exceeds that of impoverished Honduras. The United States, in less than two decades, went from being the world's largest creditor nation to being the world's largest debtor. It is also a country of stark contrasts including billionaires and homeless people, measles epidemics and military bands, crack babies and Wall Street speculators.

The most disturbing parallel between the United States and the Third World is that massive wealth transfers from the third-world poor to the first-world rich have a domestic counterpart.

During the 1980s there was a dramatic shift in wealth from poor and working-class Americans to U.S. elites. This upward redistribution of wealth was accompanied by a radical shift in relative wealth and economic power from the United States to Japan and Western Europe. There is one other paradox that is central to understanding U.S. goals within the new world order: The nation's declining economic power is accompanied by and linked to United States ascendancy as the world's undisputed leader in military power.

## Domestic Hunger and Poverty

In his reelection campaign in 1984 President Reagan asked U.S. voters whether they were better off now than they were during the previous administration. Fortunately for Reagan, and for President Bush who reached the White House in part based on the popularity of his predecessor, the poor stay away from the polls in disproportionate numbers and future generations are not allowed to vote until eighteen years after they are born.

The Reagan and Bush years produced, according to Kevin Phillips, a Republican party strategist, "one of U.S. history's most striking concentrations of wealth." This wealth concentration occurred "as the American dream was beginning to crumble not just in inner-city ghettos and farm townships but in blue collar centers and even middle-class suburbs."[1] The gap between the richest and poorest U.S. citizens is now greater than at any time since the Census Bureau began collecting such data in 1947. The poorest twenty percent of the U.S. population receive 3.8 percent of national income; the richest twenty percent get 46.1 percent.[2]

If talk of victory in the Cold War sounded bitterly ironic to poor people living in third-world countries allied with the United States, it is doubly so for people living in third-world conditions *within* the United States. The following litany of ills provides ample evidence of a nation in crisis:

• One in four children in the United States is born into poverty.

• More than thirty-five million U.S. citizens lack any type of health insurance. Millions more have only limited coverage.

• The United States ranks twenty-second in infant mortality, behind most of our industrial allies.

• Most of the poor in the United States are full-time workers or their dependents. This reflects a serious deterioration in the wages and benefits of significant sectors of the U.S. work force.

• In 1985, 20.4 percent of all infants below age 1 were not fully vaccinated against polio, 41.5 percent of infants of color.

• One-fourth of the poorest low-income households spend more than seventy-five percent of their incomes for rent.[3]

• The United States has the world's largest per capita prison population; 426 of every 100,000 people are in jail. By way of comparison, the incarceration rates per 100,000 people are 333 in South Africa, 268 in the Soviet Union, 97 in Great Britain, 76 in Spain, and 40 in the Netherlands.[4]

• The United States, according to a United Nation's Development Program report, also has the highest murder rate and highest incidence of reported rape among industrialized countries.[5]

These acute social problems are a consequence of national policies and priorities that enrich certain sectors at the expense of others. These policies include enormous tax cuts for the richest Americans, major cuts in social services, huge trade and budget deficits, and massive infusions of foreign capital. They reward speculative rather than productive investment and emphasize military production and power over socially useful production. By describing in general terms the economic changes that occurred over the past decade, and the winners and losers from these changes, we can discover the forces and constituencies giving shape to the new world order.

"America's richest 5 percent (and richest 1 percent in particular)," writes Kevin Phillips, "were the ... beneficiaries" of major changes in the U.S. tax code.[6] Tax reforms benefited the rich in several ways. The top personal tax bracket rate dropped from seventy percent to twenty-eight percent over seven years. At the same time the rate of federal tax receipts from corporate income tax revenues continued to plummet from 32.1 percent in 1952, to 12.5 percent in 1980, to an all-time low of 6.2 percent in 1983.[7] The burden of taxation shifted further onto low-income households as social security tax rate hikes accompanied lower income tax rates. According to Senator George Mitchell this resulted in "a shift of about $80 billion in annual revenue collections from the progressive income tax to the regressive payroll tax."[8] In the first five years following the passage of the 1981 Economic Recovery Tax Act the superrich "shared a half-trillion dollar victory."[9] These tax changes translated into deepening disparities between the incomes of the rich and poor. Between 1977 and 1988, according to a Congressional Budget Office report, the incomes of the wealthiest fifth of U.S. households increased thirty-four percent, the incomes of the middle fifth grew four percent and the incomes of the poorest fifth dropped by ten percent. The top one percent benefited most. Their incomes rose by 122 percent, rising from an average of $203,000 in 1977 to $451,000 in 1988.[10] According to the 1991 *Green Book* from the House Ways and Means Committee, the after-tax income of the richest one percent of all U.S. citizens in 1988 was as great as the combined after-tax income of the bottom forty percent. By way of contrast, the after-tax income of the bottom forty percent in 1977 was more than double the total after-tax income of the richest one percent.[11]

In addition to tax breaks for the rich the Reagan administration increased military spending by thirty-eight percent from 1982 through 1986.[12] Burgeoning military expenditures further traumatized the federal budget, which had already lost hundreds of billions of dollars of potential tax revenues. The results were huge deficits that drained the federal budget because of rising interest payments. Annual federal expenditures on interest for the federal debt rose from $96 billion in 1981 to $216 billion in 1988.[13]

The policies that led to unprecedented wealth for the richest Americans and renewed power for the military industrial complex resulted in a budget deficit "crisis." Ironically, this budget crisis itself offered additional profit opportunities for the rich. However, the crisis was real and immediate for the poor. It shackled both present and future generations of poor and working-class Americans who bore—and will bear—the weight of elite imposed "solutions."

Tax breaks for the rich, military spending increases, and rising interest payments were paid for in part by substantial cuts in programs that most directly benefited the poor. During 1982-86, a period of huge military expenditures and concentrated wealth, there were dramatic cuts in social programs. Federal spending, corrected for inflation, included budget cuts in the following areas:

| | |
|---|---|
| housing | 82% |
| employment and training | 52% |
| mass transit | 28% |
| community development | 20% |
| education | 14% |
| AFDC (Families with Dependent Children) | 11% |
| health | 8%[14] |

In addition the federal food stamp program was cut $6.8 billion from FY 1982 to FY 1985.[15]

U.S. policies border on economic apartheid as U.S. elites, like their third-world counterparts, impose austerity measures on the poor. Most graphically, as economic opportunities and federally funded housing units are severely limited by budget cuts the poor find "alternative housing" in prisons. The United States not only has the highest rate of imprisonment of any nation in the world, it has the most racially biased prison system. One of four black males is in the criminal justice system—in jail, on trial, awaiting trial or on parole. South Africa's incarceration rate for blacks is 729 per 100,000. The U.S. rate is 3,109.[16] If present trends continue, shortly after the middle of the next century one-half of all U.S. citizens will be in jail!

The poor are not the only sector to bear the weight of tax policies, military expenditures, and the resulting budget deficit crisis. In 1988 nearly one-half of *all* personal income tax receipts were used just to pay the interest on the national debt.[17] Huge deficits impose a tax burden on present and future generations of Americans, who will be paying for recent economic folly for decades to come. General taxpayers are also paying for individual and corporate greed through the publicly financed bailout of the Savings and Loan (S & L) Industry. The Bush administration estimated in 1990 that the S & L bailout will cost $400 billion, or $1,600 for every man, woman, and child in the United

States.[18] A broader banking crisis could cost much more as funds in the Federal Deposit Insurance Corporation are rapidly depleted. "As many as 440 banks may fail this year and in 1992," *The New York Times* reported in June 1991, "costing the insurance fund $23 billion and leaving it with a deficit of nearly $6 billion next year."[19]

Funding the deficit further realigns the nation's wealth because it provides additional profit opportunities for the rich. It also diverts funds from health care, education, environmental cleanup, and socially useful production. Senator Patrick Moynihan notes that huge interest payments on the national debt involve a transfer of wealth from labor to capital that is unprecedented in American history. Eighty percent of the federal interest payments went to the upper twenty percent of U.S. income earners, who, because of generous tax breaks, paid lower taxes on these earnings.[20]

It is not enough to say that huge budget deficits are bad. The important question is, bad for whom? U.S. economic policies and military priorities lead to massive budget deficits that hurt poor and working-class Americans while undermining the nation's economy. However, huge deficits are "tactical pluses" for the rich. "They *did*," Phillips notes, "help fund the tax cuts; they *did* keep real interest rates high [high interest rates are needed to attract the foreign capital that keeps the U.S. government afloat]; and they *did* squeeze discretionary federal domestic spending to a latter-day record-low percentage of GNP" (emphasis in original).[21] In short, the budget deficits helped finance the upward redistribution of wealth and the dramatic increase in military spending. They also ensured the economic decline of the country relative to Japan and Western Europe, an important link in understanding the U.S. role in the new world order.

## Economic Decline

"The most important story about the U.S. economy in the eighties," David Gordon of the New School of Social Research said, "is the economic warfare that the wealthy and powerful have been waging against the vast majority of Americans."[22] The consequences of this warfare are graphically illustrated above: impoverished children, hunger, homelessness, declining quality of jobs, expanded prisons, and social cutbacks. The United States ranks twenty-second in infant mortality, but number one in rates of rape, murder, and incarceration. It is first in global debt, and number one in weapons sales to third-world countries, but is one of only two industrialized countries (South Africa being the other) without comprehensive national health systems.

The measurements of U.S. economic decline go beyond social indicators and comparisons. The ultimate casualty in the war waged by the U.S. wealthy against poor and working-class Americans is the U.S. economy itself. U.S. elites sacrifice the country's economic health to their own greed and profits. Structural changes that have seriously eroded U.S. economic power relative to Western Europe and Japan are at the root of U.S. economic decline.

The post–Cold War new world order is taking shape in a tripolar world in which there is significant economic rivalry. Each of the leading powers—the United States, Japan, and Western Europe—is forming economic zones of influence with itself at the center. The United States, the weakest of the three major economic powers, is consolidating its regional economic influence through alliances with Canada, Mexico, and the countries of Latin America and the Caribbean. The European Economic Community is removing significant barriers to the movement of people, capital, goods, and services. It is creating "the world's most prosperous single market, with 323 million people."[23] Western Europe is further expanding its power and influence through ties to the newly independent and economically vulnerable countries of Eastern Europe and with third-world nations in the Mediterranean basin. Japan, whose influence is global by virtue of its wealth, is nonetheless busily consolidating its regional power base. Economist Walden Bello notes:

> Indeed, we might witness over the next decade the first stages of an East Asian division of labor centered on Japan, with China and Southeast Asia providing the cheap labor; the Soviet Union, China, and Southeast Asia the

natural resources; and Japan and, to some degree, the NICs [newly industrialized countries, especially Taiwan and South Korea] providing the markets, technology, and capital. This geoeconomic revolution . . . would have massive geopolitical consequences. . . . One of the main consequences would be the acceleration of U.S. economic decline.[24]

The economic decline of the United States is linked to two fundamental problems. First, debt-induced prosperity results in massive transfers of wealth to foreigners and leads to major foreign ownership of U.S. businesses and real estate. Second, U.S. "prosperity" isn't rooted in productive investment. As a result "the dominant trend is the passage of economic and technological primacy from the United States to Japan."[25]

In the 1980s rich Americans grew wealthier by mortgaging the financial health of the country. U.S. international indebtedness was approximately $269 billion at the end of 1986, reached $368 billion at the end of 1987, and was expected to exceed $1 trillion in 1992. Kevin Phillips describes how tax cuts and budget deficits resulted in a dramatic transfer of wealth from the United States to Japan:

Tax cuts certainly benefited many individuals, but at a grave price. Growing federal budget and trade deficits have forced the United States to borrow heavily from overseas, and after 1985, the value of the dollar plummeted, resulting in an extraordinary realignment of world wealth and purchasing power — and possibly standards of living. Between 1985 and 1987 the total national assets of the United States climbed from $30.6 trillion to $36.2 trillion while those of Japan, just $19.6 trillion in 1985, soared to $43.7 trillion in 1987, an almost unimaginable transfer of relative wealth and purchasing power from the United States to Japan.[26]

The United States resembles a third-world country in its economic relations with its Western partners. Like indebted third-world countries, the United States increasingly depends on and is vulnerable to foreign creditors. U.S. interest rates are kept high to attract foreign capital, austerity measures are imposed on the poor, wages for U.S. workers are pushed lower, and foreigners control important sectors of the U.S. economy. Cumulative direct foreign investment in U.S. corporations and real estate increased from $83 billion in 1980 to $304 billion in 1988. As of 1988 foreigners owned twelve percent of America's manufacturing base, up from three percent in 1980.[27] By 1988, according to the Coldwell Banker Real Estate Group, foreigners owned forty-six percent of Los Angeles's commercial real estate, thirty-nine percent of downtown Houston's; thirty-two percent of Minneapolis's and twenty-one percent of Manhattan's.[28]

U.S. debt and deficits give foreigners substantial leverage over the U.S. economy and claims on future U.S. priorities and resources. However, there is another related and important factor fueling U.S. economic decline: the United States is practicing a type of "casino capitalism" in which "prosperity" is based on speculation and paper wealth and not on productive investment. Throughout the 1980s debt-induced prosperity was achieved at the expense of real productivity. A financial columnist for the *Philadelphia Inquirer* noted similarities between the economic situation of 1986 and the 1920s:

> Then as now, banks, investment houses and brokerage firms created the debt that made money-making excursions in Wall Street possible. Money was used primarily to make money, not to produce goods and services and raise people's living standards.[29]

Many of those who benefited from the wealth orgy of the 1980s were "people who packaged the new financial and debt instruments proliferating on every side. Others," Kevin Phillips notes, "made money by the corporate raiding and reshuffling encouraged by Reagan-era regulatory permissivism and global pressures. Moving or refinancing assets was easier than building or manufacturing them."[30]

The problems associated with nonproductive investment are aggravated by the emphasis on military-related production. Decades of huge military expenditures, including a dramatic increase in military spending in the 1980s, shifted dollars away from social services. They also further drained the U.S. economy of other socially useful investments and production. Seymour Melman summarizes the relationship between military production and U.S. economic decline:

> While the arms race with its unspeakable hazards proceeds, it has generated a catastrophe in slow motion for the American people. The United States has been transformed into a second rate industrial economy. The Pentagon degraded the growth of efficiency in US industry, first by replacing cost-minimizing with cost-maximizing as a main managerial method. Second, by preempting trillions of dollars of capital resources since World War II the Pentagon drained off real wealth from productive use, finally proving even American wealth has limits.[31]

As euphoria over the outcome of the Gulf War swept through the country the Council on Competitiveness, a nonprofit organization of top U.S. business, education, and labor leaders, issued a sobering report on the United States' economic future. The Council's report described how a decade ago the United States dominated the area of high technology but was now losing badly to foreigners. "America's once-commanding lead in the critical technologies driving economic growth and national security," the report stated, "is being seriously challenged by foreign competitors." In one-third of the critical technologies U.S. companies were so far behind that they either were no longer a factor in world markets or they were expected to fall hopelessly behind over the next five years.[32]

The declining competitive position of the U.S. economy is a widely acknowledged problem among business and government leaders. However, there are different approaches to restoring the competitiveness of the U.S. economy. The most pragmatic approach would require a fundamental shift in the priorities of research and investment. Another option is to try to make U.S. goods and services internationally competitive by devaluing the dollar. This approach was tried in the mid-1980s. It resulted in a massive foreign takeover of U.S. businesses and real estate.

U.S. goods became somewhat more competitive but at the expense of the economic sovereignty of the country. Another way to improve one's competitive position is to reduce the wages and living standards of workers. Ironically, in 1985 the President's Commission on Industrial Competitiveness ruled out that approach, which is now central to U.S. economic strategy within the new world order:

> Competitiveness is the degree to which a nation can, under free and fair market conditions, produce goods and services that meet the test of international markets while simultaneously maintaining or expanding the real incomes of its citizens. . . . It is not our goal to compete by decreasing the real incomes of our people. *Other nations may compete by having low wage levels, but that is not an option America would choose.* [Emphasis added.][33]

Restoring the competitive position of the United States would require a major revision of the tax code to encourage productive investment, a dramatic shift of resources out of the military sector, and huge investments in the education and health of our people. These changes also would require challenging the groups that dominate the new world order. Clearly, the goal of the United States within the new order is to improve the competitive position of the United States at the expense of U.S. and foreign workers. According to *Forbes*:

> Over the next 20 years, the U.S. could face a severe labour shortage. Mexico by contrast has at least 5 million unemployed workers and will add as many as a million job seekers in each of the next five years. That's ten million workers willing to work for $1 an hour, available to add value to U.S. produced goods and services and to keep U.S. products world-competitive. It is not important whether the Mexicans work in the U.S. or in U.S.-owned factories in Mexico. The important thing is that a better way be found to marry U.S. investment with Mexican labour.[34]

The "labour shortage" in the United States is, of course, a shortage of workers willing to work for a dollar an hour. "Until we get real wage levels down much closer to those of the Brazils and Koreas," a vice president of the Goodyear Corporation said, "We cannot pass along productivity gains to wages and still be competitive."[35]

The benefits to U.S. corporations from poorly paid foreign workers go beyond the goods they produce. Foreign wages of one dollar an hour push U.S. wages lower and therefore make the U.S. economy "more competitive." The fact that the majority of poor people in the United States are full-time workers or their dependents signals an already serious decline in wages and benefits. In 1985 seventy percent of the uninsured were full-time, full-year workers or their families. A minimum-wage job today pays seventy-one percent of the federal poverty line for a family of three. In the 1960s a minimum-wage job lifted a family above the poverty line.[36] Weekly wages for U.S. workers in the fall of 1988 were 2.4 percent below 1980 levels and were falling at a rate of more than one percent a year. The Government Accounting Office has reported in virtually all sections of the country the resurgence of sweatshops—businesses that violate wage, child labor, safety, and health laws.[37]

At the same time wages for U.S. workers have declined, those of corporate executives have soared. In 1990 Chrysler Chief Lee Iacocca's pay package totaled $4.6 million. He received a twenty-five percent increase in pay while Chrysler executives called for cost-saving concessions from workers and while company earnings declined seventy-nine percent. In 1960 it took the combined salaries of forty-one factory workers to equal the salary of the average corporate executive officer (CEO). In 1988 it took the combined salaries of eighty-five workers.[38]

The earlier discussion of third-world poverty and the role of the IMF makes clear that exploitation of underdeveloped countries is a central feature of the new world order. Free-trade agreements between the United States and other weaker economic partners such as Mexico are a means by which U.S. corporations can capitalize on cheap labor costs in order to improve their competitive position. The United States is confident that third-world indebtedness will provide the United States with permanent leverage over third-world economies and workers. SAP provisions, such as currency devaluations, will ensure that

U.S. corporations never experience a "labour shortage" in Mexico. Free-trade agreements will also accelerate the already disturbing trend of U.S. companies seeking to become competitive by lowering the living standards of U.S. workers.

In the 1980s the rich grew richer and the military more powerful through governmental policies that impoverished the country and slashed social programs and spending. The individual and corporate greed that fueled these policies aggravated numerous social problems. Hunger, homelessness, deteriorating education and health care, drug epidemics, and burgeoning prison populations were some of the negative social by-products of the period. Ironically, these social problems also contribute to the deterioration of the U.S. economy. The Committee for Economic Development, in a report entitled *Children in Need: Investment Strategies for the Economically Disadvantaged*, notes:

> This nation cannot continue to compete and prosper in the global arena when more than one-fifth of our children live in poverty and a third grow up in ignorance. And if the nation cannot compete, it cannot lead. If we continue to squander the talents of millions of our children America will become a nation of limited human potential. It would be tragic if we allow this to happen. America must become a land of opportunity—for every child.[39]

## Conclusion

The United States and the world stood at a critical threshold as the Cold War came to an end. As poverty took a brutal toll on people throughout the Third World, poor countries transferred unprecedented wealth to developed countries. Locked into a cycle of poverty and indebtedness, most third-world peoples saw living standards erode throughout the decade of the eighties. Economic growth was down while infant mortality, malnutrition, and despair were up. The U.S. economy was also deteriorating as elite U.S. sectors grew rich at the expense of the country. During the 1980s the gap between the rich and the poor grew to obscene proportions. The weight of policies that stressed military priorities over socially useful production, and spiralling and concentrated paper wealth for the few at the expense of the majority of poor and working-class citizens, seriously eroded the living standards of many Americans and undermined the U.S. economy. Both the U.S. poor and the U.S. economy closed out the decade in a precarious position. The poor were marginalized relative to the broader society. The U.S. economy was marginalized relative to the economies of Japan and Western Europe.

The end of the Cold War should have been greeted with a chorus of alleluias. Songs of praise were warranted because the Cold War thaw offered hope that something new was possible, not only for people in Eastern Europe but for U.S. and third-world peoples shackled by poverty and economic inequality. The end of superpower rivalry offered hope to third-world countries long held hostage by the dominant powers, who refused to allow nonalignment.

The end of the Cold War also offered hope for the United States, where economic problems were well advanced but not terminal. Judicious use of hundreds of billions of dollars of savings from the long-awaited "peace dividend," coupled with major tax, economic, and social reforms, offered possibilities for hope and revitalization. The world was standing at the threshold of a new world order. Unfortunately, the possibility of an authentically new order threatened entrenched interests and was quickly dashed. The possibility of meaningful reforms lay dead in the sand, a premeditated casualty of the Gulf War. It was replaced with a "brave new world order" that suited elite U.S. interests. As President Bush's popularity soared and as the nation reveled in its "victory," a tragic symbol of the new order quietly struggled to enter our consciousness: amid daily articles praising U.S. military technology and war-making capabilities there were reports of a measles epidemic sweeping through the United States while an epidemic of cholera spread through Peru to other Latin American countries. U.S. militarism had triumphed. There was a role for the United States in the post–Cold War period that didn't involve offending the military-industrial complex, addressing third-world poverty, reforming the U.S. economy, or redistributing wealth. The new world order, rooted in the injustice of the old, apparently needed a global military enforcer. The U.S. National Security Establishment would lead the country down a deadly path as it carved out a niche for the United States in the aftermath of the Cold War.

CHAPTER 3

# National Security State Doctrine

# and the New World Order

*Women and men have shed their blood — people from El Salvador, from Spain, and from the United States. People from different confessions, from different faiths, from different places, are united in their soul, as we all are by the tragedy in El Salvador and also by the hope and the commitment of the martyrs. We all know why these people ended in the cross, why they were killed. They dared "touch the idols of death."*
*. . . Archbishop Oscar Romero of El Salvador defined idols as the accumulation of wealth and the doctrine of national security. Those who dare touch these idols get killed.*
— Jon Sobrino, *Sojourners,*
February-March 1990

The end of the Cold War offered new possibilities to the nation and to the world. The old order, which had been dominated by superpower rivalries, was rapidly evolving in new directions. The dynamics shaping the new order included the decline of the Soviet Union, the economic supremacy of Europe and Japan, the military supremacy and economic decline of the United States, and poverty-induced political instability in many third-world countries considered strategic to the West.

As the Cold War ended the U.S. economy was cracking under

33

the weight of growing contradictions between military power and social decay. The United States desperately needed to reorder priorities and to make judicious use of a post–Cold War "peace dividend" to begin a process of domestic economic and social renewal. Instead, the United States with stunning speed shaped a world order in which new enemies were found, the "peace dividend" evaporated, and the military reasserted its primacy in American life.

The end of the Cold War offered two distinct paths to the future. The U.S. National Security Establishment, with presidential leadership, forsook economic revitalization in favor of militarism. How and why did this happen? In Chapter 7 I will discuss the specific role of the Gulf crisis in the formation of a so-called new world order that caters to the interests of the U.S. National Security Establishment. However, before doing so it is important to place the paths chosen (militarism) and not chosen (economic revitalization) in the context of a broader discussion about the dynamics and dangers of a National Security State. That is the purpose of this and the following chapter.

## Dangerous Features

Archbishop Romero called National Security doctrine an idol. Those who "touch" or unmask the dominant place of this idol within society, including Romero himself, are killed. What is meant by "National Security doctrine" or a "National Security State"? It is difficult to define precisely a National Security State or its ideology because, as José Comblin notes in *The Church and the National Security State*, it "has no official name."[1] Comblin identifies a number of characteristics of a National Security State or National Security State ideology including: setting legal or functional limits on constitutional authority; justifying human rights and other abuses committed by agents of the state by appealing to higher values or to the defense of the state itself; seeking national unity based on attacks against external or internal enemies; and the lodging of ultimate state power in military hands.[2]

I believe that we cannot understand the significance of the Gulf War and the role of the United States in the new world order without comprehending the dangers and dynamics of a National Security State. Building on Comblin's work and based on my experience of life and politics in Central America and the United States, I have identified seven characteristics of a National Security State or National Security doctrine. Each of the seven characteristics is readily visible in a U.S. client state like El Salvador, so following the summary of each characteristic is a brief description of how it finds expression in El Salvador. Exploring the dynamics of a National Security State in El Salvador can help us understand similar dynamics operating within the United States. As I will demonstrate below and in the following chapters, the Gulf War and the new world order are products of the U.S. National Security State Establishment.

*The first characteristic of a National Security State is that the military is the highest authority.* In a National Security State the military not only guarantees the security of the state against all internal and external enemies, it has enough power to determine the overall direction of the society. In a National Security State the military exerts important influence over political, economic, as well as military affairs.

The military has dominated life in El Salvador for generations. Over the past decade it has dramatically increased its power as a result of billions of dollars in U.S. aid. The military in El Salvador, apart from the U.S. embassy, is clearly the highest authority in the country. Its power flows from its close ties to the United States, its institutional presence and capacity for violence throughout the country, its relationship to paramilitary death squads, its ability to control and intimidate a weak judicial system, and its dominant political and economic influence.[3]

*A second defining feature of a National Security State is that political democracy and democratic elections are viewed with suspicion, contempt, or in terms of political expediency. National Security States often maintain an appearance of democracy. However, ultimate power rests with the military or within a broader National Security Establishment.*

If the military is the highest authority in a country (the first feature of a National Security State), then this precludes the possibility of authentic democracy. Elections are nonetheless important. Elections in El Salvador have performed a key function *on behalf of the National Security State*: They "legitimize" the state without changing basic power realities. Salvadoran elections are carried out in a context of psychological warfare (including managed terror), foreign domination, military abuses, and a nonfunctional judicial system. Ignacio Martin-Baro from the Catholic University explains why elections should not be equated with democracy:

> According to an image widely circulated by U.S. government spokespersons, El Salvador represents the best example of the "new Latin American democracies.". . . Regrettably, this image of the country reflects little, if anything, of the real situation of El Salvador. The democratic character of a government does not depend—at least not solely—on the way in which it is elected, but rather on the forces that determine its day-to-day conduct. And the verifiable fact is that, in terms of El Salvador's basic policies, North American fears about "national security" count more than the most basic needs of the Salvadoran people. It would never cross any Salvadoran's mind that the . . . government might have some significant control over the Salvadoran armed forces: this is simply the result of the daily experience of Salvadorans of who is in charge there.[4]

A central feature of U.S. "low-intensity conflict" strategy, as I documented in *War Against the Poor*, is using elections to cover up the militarization of societies.[5] In that earlier book I quoted a priest, whom I didn't name out of concern for his safety. His name was Ignacio Martin-Baro, one of the six Jesuits murdered at the Catholic University in San Salvador in November 1989. "The U.S. project is not democracy," he told me. "The U.S. project is to use 'democracy' to muffle international criticism in order better to control El Salvador. 'Democracy' is a facade to cover many unpleasant things." One of the unpleasant things it covered up was his own brutal murder.

*A third characteristic of a National Security State is that the military and related sectors wield substantial political and economic power. They do so in the context of an ideology which stresses that "freedom" and "development" are possible only when capital is concentrated in the hands of elites.*

Money and wealth-producing resources are generally concentrated within three sectors: the private business sector, the state or state enterprise sector, and within the military itself. The state facilitates capital accumulation and manages tensions between these elite sectors, sets the boundaries of such accumulation by acknowledging minimal social constraints to unimpeded greed, and manages resulting social tensions. In other words, the state sets out to benefit elites, justifies its policies through appeals to broader goals of "freedom" and "development," recognizes that misery can lead to social rebellion, and responds to social tensions through accommodation or repression.

This portrayal of the role of the state is, in many ways, a description of politics in most Western societies. Politics has a central role to play in determining the distribution of wealth and power. However, *in National Security States the military and related sectors directly or indirectly exercise tremendous influence over political and economic affairs.* One of the ironies of U.S. policy is that through the police functions of the IMF the United States encourages concentration of capital in the private sector. However, the overall impact of its foreign policy is to ensure the predominance of military priorities, which leads to the militarization of societies.

The role of the state in facilitating the concentration of wealth on behalf of economic elites is an ongoing feature of life in El Salvador. However, a particularly disturbing feature of El Salvador's National Security State is the degree to which sectors of the U.S.-backed military dominate economic and political life. Over the past decade the Salvadoran military has gotten rich from the war. U.S. preoccupation with "national security" and its support for the military within El Salvador's National Security State have made the Salvadoran military a leading *political and economic power.*

The Salvadoran military, with support from the United States, has used its political control to block a negotiated settlement to the country's civil war. A negotiated settlement, although favored by almost every other sector of Salvadoran society, including some sectors of the non-military-based economic elite, would reduce the military's political and economic power. In an April 1990 report entitled "El Salvador: Is Peace Possible," the Washington Office on Latin America (WOLA) states:

> Despite the presence of some moderate officers . . . successful pursuit of a negotiated settlement would directly threaten the interests of individual officers as well as those of their institution. . . . Within the officer corps . . . the arguments against negotiations remain persuasive: First, any reduction in troop size as a result of negotiations would necessitate a corresponding reduction in the officer corps. . . . Second, as the Armed Forces have expanded in size and wealth because of the war, so too has their influence. *By any estimate, the military stands as the country's single most powerful social and economic institution.* It distributes a large part of U.S. economic aid in hearts and minds campaigns run as an integral part of military operations. It has set up a social security fund, believed to have more than $100 million. . . . The military has invested in a wide range of business and real estate ventures. Consequently, *any progress toward a negotiated settlement would challenge the military's privileged position within the government and society.* [Emphasis added.][6]

*A fourth feature of a National Security State is its obsession with enemies.* There are enemies of the state everywhere. Defending against external and/or internal enemies becomes a leading preoccupation of the state, a distorting factor in the economy, and a major source of national identity and purpose.

In El Salvador there is no shortage of enemies: independent unions and union leaders, students, campesino groups demanding land reform and access to credit, teachers, grass-roots health workers, human rights groups and organizers, independent journalists, and progressive churches and church workers are all enemies of the state. They refuse to accept the inevitability of a National Security State, and therefore they organize for democratic and economic reforms. The state lumps all opposition groups together with the armed opposition in El Salvador, the FMLN (Faribundo Marti National Liberation Front). In general, enemies in El Salvador have been defined by the National Security State as internal groups linked to an "international communist movement" spearheaded by the Soviet Union, Cuba, and Nicaragua.

*A fifth ideological foundation of a National Security State is that the enemies of the state are cunning and ruthless. Therefore, any means used to destroy or control these enemies is justified.*

Bishops and priests get murdered, campesinos are massacred, labor leaders and human rights workers disappeared and are tortured in El Salvador because the "enemies" of the National Security State have ceased to be human. "Enemies of the state" are being eliminated, not people. "Communists" are being killed, not human beings. Shortly before the murder of the two women and six Jesuits at the Catholic University in San Salvador the U.S.-trained Salvadoran Air Force produced and distributed a leaflet saying:

> Salvadoran Patriot! You have the . . . right to defend your life and property. If in order to do that you must kill FMLN terrorists as well as their "internationalist" allies, do it. . . . Let's destroy them. Let's finish them off. With God, reason, and might, we shall conquer.

The day after the murders, soldiers of San Salvador's First Infantry Brigade circled the office of the Catholic archdiocese in a military sound truck, shouting: "Ignacio Ellacuría and Ignacio Martin-Baro have already fallen and we will continue murdering communists."[7]

*A sixth characteristic of a National Security State is that it restricts public debate and limits popular participation through secrecy or intimidation.* Authentic democracy depends on participation of the people. National Security States limit such participation in a number of ways: They sow fear and thereby narrow the range of public debate; they restrict and distort information; and they define policies in secret and implement those policies through covert channels and clandestine activities. The state justifies such actions through rhetorical pleas of "higher purpose" and vague appeals to "national security."

Secrecy takes many forms in El Salvador. Over the past decade the U.S. embassy has managed many aspects of the war and the economy. This fact, known by most Salvadorans, is "secret" because it compromises national sovereignty. So also is the relationship between death squads and key elements of the Salvadoran military and government. Secrecy in this case is vital to the National Security State's maintenance of a facade of democratic rule.

In El Salvador's National Security State "citizen participation" and "democracy" are seriously compromised by death squads, spy networks, and military intimidation. A climate of fear pervades the society. Ignacio Martin-Baro surveyed 250 refugees in one settlement on the outskirts of San Salvador. He found that "the presence of the army in the vicinity of the refuge was sufficient to cause 87 percent of those questioned to experience fear; 75 percent felt an accelerated pulse rate, and 64 percent were overcome by generalized bodily trembling."[8]

State-sponsored terrorist attacks against alternative media sources further restrict information and debate. "From January 6, 1976 ... when they placed the first bomb in our university," Jon Sobrino wrote in November 1989, "there have been fifteen occasions when bombs have been planted, in the print room, the computer center, the library, the administration building. The last one exploded on July 22 ... partially destroying the printing press."[9] *Diario Latino*, the only opposition newspaper in El Salvador, was seriously damaged by arson on February 9, 1991, shortly after President Bush announced his intention to unfreeze $42.5 million in aid to the Salvadoran military.

*Finally, the church is expected to mobilize its financial, ideological, and theological resources in service to the National Security State.* This helps explain why persecution of progressive churches is a common feature within many National Security States.

Religious persecution, according to *America's Watch*, is an ongoing feature of life in El Salvador.[10] This is illustrated by the assassination of Archbishop Romero in 1980, the rape and murder of U.S. church women that same year, the deaths of hundreds of lay church workers from base Christian communities throughout the past decade, the brutal murders of the Jesuits, and continued repression and intimidation directed at the churches in the aftermath of the Jesuit murders.

El Salvador's National Security State apparatus is still trying to kill the spirit of resistance and the Spirit of God embodied in the life and example of Archbishop Romero. The U.S.-trained forces that entered the Catholic University and murdered the two women and the Jesuits also destroyed two portraits of Romero. They shot a bullet through the heart of one Romero portrait and apparently destroyed the other with a flame thrower.

## Conclusion

This summary of the essential characteristics of a National Security State elicits responses that range from disbelief to horror. Those who see U.S. policy in El Salvador as promoting democracy are obviously offended. Others shake their heads and breathe a sigh of relief. "This is awful," they say, "but I'm glad I don't live in a National Security State." Others, more uncomfortable still, recognize that El Salvador's National Security State is a product of U.S. policy. They are troubled by apparent contradictions between our internal conduct as a nation and our nation's foreign policy, which encourages such abuses. Finally, there are people who see many of the characteristics of a National Security State operating within the United States. It is this ominous insight that holds the key to unlocking the mystery of the Gulf crisis and the new world order.

Ironically, there may be light at the end of a very dark tunnel in El Salvador, where people recognize the dangers of a National Security State and creatively struggle to wrest power away from the military. The peoples' efforts may succeed in reducing the power of the military and replacing the National Security State dominated order with something new. The same may be said for the Soviet Union where in August 1991 the people successfully thwarted a coup and thereby took an important step toward democracy. The prospects for the U.S. people may be bleaker. It seems we have entered the dark tunnel of a National Security State unaware and unconcerned, too busy waving flags to be bothered with the erosion of our democracy.

## CHAPTER 4

# The U.S. National Security State

*In the councils of government we must guard against the acquisition of unwarranted influence, whether sought or unsought, by the military-industrial complex. The potential for the disastrous rise of misplaced power exists and will persist.*
—President Dwight D. Eisenhower

In the late 1970s José Comblin, a Belgian theologian who lived in Latin America since the early 1950s, detailed the relationship between the U.S. and Latin American National Security States. "The Latin American nations have copied the United States in creating similar institutions," Comblin noted, "and have followed their ideology to its logical conclusions with devastating results."[1] The United States, according to Comblin, exported and then adapted its own National Security State institutions to countries like El Salvador. If this is true then the dangers and dynamics of a National Security State so evident in El Salvador will likely be manifested in similar ways within the United States.

### Formation of a National Security State

The U.S. National Security Establishment firmly took root in the aftermath of World War II. The United States emerged from the war as *the* global power. Its economy and military were intact in a world largely destroyed by war. The United States used its privileged position to establish a massive network of foreign military bases and to shape a world order conducive to its economic interests.

U.S. national security interests became increasingly global in scope, and they were closely identified with maintaining existing global inequalities. George Kennan, who headed the State Department's planning staff in 1948, warned that the United States would be "the object of envy and resentment" because it had "about 50% of the world's wealth, but only 6.3% of its population." The goal of the United States in the emerging world order, Kennan stated, was "to devise a pattern of relationships which will permit us to maintain this position of disparity without positive detriment to our national security." In order to maintain this disparity and defend U.S. national security, the United States had "to cease to talk about vague and ... unreal objectives such as human rights, the raising of living standards and democratization." Instead, he noted, the United States had "to deal in straight power concepts."[2]

The United States, according to Kennan's description of the prevailing worldview, was a global power in a hostile world. The enemies of the United States included all those forces who challenged the inequities of the U.S. dominated post–World War II order. The "communist threat" became a generic symbol for all enemies, real and imagined. A secret report prepared for the White House in 1954 stated:

> It is now clear that we are facing an implacable enemy whose avowed objective is world domination. . . . There are no rules in such a game. Hitherto accepted norms of human conduct do not apply. . . . If the United States is to survive, long-standing American concepts of fair play must be reconsidered. . . . We must learn to subvert, sabotage and destroy our enemies by more clever, sophisticated, more effective methods than those used against us.[3]

The U.S. Congress established new institutions to defend the country's expanding "national" interests following World War II. In 1947 it passed the National Security Act, which created a National Security State apparatus centered around the National

Security Council (NSC) and the Central Intelligence Agency (CIA). These organs of the National Security State were dangerous for two reasons. First, *national security* is a vague term, often cited and easily abused. Defending national security became the standard justification for new weapons systems and huge military expenditures. It also rationalized numerous U.S. interventions in third-world countries and justified U.S. support for repressive National Security States throughout Latin America. In 1953 Dwight D. Eisenhower, former general and World War II hero, called attention to the inherent conflict between "guns" and "butter." "Every gun that is made," he said in his now famous quotation, "every warship launched, every rocket fired signifies, in the final sense, is a theft from those who hunger and are not fed, those who are cold and are not clothed."[4] However, the actual policy of the United States during the Eisenhower administration was to encourage military-run states that bought guns instead of butter while defending U.S. interests. In 1954 most of the thirteen Latin American presidents who were military officers were receiving military assistance from the United States. That same year Eisenhower authorized the overthrow of a democratically elected government in Guatemala that was committed to land reform, and he presented the Legion of Merit award to two Latin American dictators—Perez Jimenez of Venezuela (for his "spirit of friendship and cooperation" and his "sound foreign investment policies"), and Manuel Odria of Peru.

Thirty years later President Reagan justified disastrous and deadly U.S. policies in Central America by telling the U.S. Congress that "the national security of all the Americas is at stake." He went on to frame the choice confronting members of Congress in a manner consistent with most debates about "national security": support administration policy or risk the nation's destruction. "Who among us," he asked, "would wish to bear responsibility for failing to meet our shared obligation?"[5]

National Security State institutions like the NSC and CIA are also dangerous because they greatly expand the power of the executive branch and thereby threaten the constitutional system of checks and balances. The institutions that make up the National Security State apparatus are supposedly set up to defend national security and the integrity of the state. However, they often abuse power, violate national and international laws, and may actually erode the democracy they supposedly defend. Senate investigations led by Frank Church in 1975 detailed numerous illegal activities conducted by the CIA against U.S. and foreign individuals and groups. The recent Iran-Contra scandal, discussed below, offers frightening testimony to abuses of power by the National Security Council, including numerous violations of the U.S. Constitution.

The CIA and the NSC are but two elements in the U.S. National Security Establishment. The post–World War II world order established by the United States required huge military expenditures, constantly updated and improved weapons systems, and costly interventionism. Important sectors of the U.S. economy, lured by huge and easy profits, became dependent on military contracts and the Pentagon. This led, in President Eisenhower's phrase, to a "military-industrial complex," a loose network of military officers, industrial managers, and legislators who all had a vested interest in permanent, high military expenditures. This military-industrial complex together with national security agencies such as the NSC and CIA make up what I call the National Security Establishment.

The features of a National Security State so evident in El Salvador now threaten the integrity of U.S. democracy and the long-term health of the U.S. economy. The preoccupation with internal enemies at various points in our nation's history has seriously limited the parameters of domestic debate and dissent. U.S. politics, in many ways, still take place under McCarthy's shadow. The focus on external enemies led to the formation of a National Security Establishment. This group not only helped the United States to create and support National Security States throughout much of the Third World but came to exercise tremendous influence over U.S. domestic economic and political affairs. It has a vested interest in finding new enemies and fears the prospect of a peace dividend. Unfortunately, it is now powerful enough to determine the overall direction of U.S. society.

"In the councils of government," President Eisenhower warned in his 1961 farewell speech to the nation, "we must guard against the acquisition of unwarranted influence, whether sought or unsought, by the military-industrial complex. The potential for the disastrous rise of misplaced power exists and will persist."

## Disturbing Signs of a U.S. National Security State

Throughout the 1980s El Salvador clearly manifested the features of a National Security State. The military was the most powerful sector of the society; it dominated political and economic life and used its power to maximize its institutional privileges; its power was sufficient to delay or derail negotiations that threatened its political and economic power; its obsession with enemies militarized the society; the tactics it used to fight perceived enemies eroded democracy within; and the National Security State it defended dramatically clashed with progressive sectors of the church.

Many of these features of a National Security State are also evident in the United States, although they sometimes find expression in different ways. One area of difference, which raises important questions to be addressed in the final two chapters, is the relationship between the church and the National Security State. Segments of the church in El Salvador have challenged the National Security State and therefore have been persecuted. Although U.S. government agencies have infiltrated churches involved in offering sanctuary to Central American refugees, the church in the United States is generally an institution of the dominating culture, which wittingly or unwittingly supports the U.S. National Security State. The church is seduced rather than repressed as religious critics are marginalized in a climate of genuine embrace between church and state.

The role of the media is another apparent difference between the National Security States of El Salvador and the United States. The Salvadoran state uses violence and terror to intimidate or silence major progressive information outlets such as *El Diario* or the presses at the Catholic University. The mainline media in the United States, like the church, are instruments of conformity within the dominating society. This conformity isn't achieved through terror and intimidation, as in El Salvador, but there is conformity nonetheless.[6] This can be illustrated by a look at coverage of the Gulf War.

The war in the Gulf was probably the most censored and media-managed war in U.S. history. The Pentagon launched the war to coincide with the evening news, forced reporters into escorted press pools, banned coverage on U.S. soldiers returning in coffins, blacked out the first forty-eight hours of the ground war, provided selective footage of "smart bombs" hitting their targets with precision, exercised the right of approval over final copy and footage, and flew local reporters in to cover selected "hometown troops."[7] "I've never seen anything to compare to it," said *New York Times* war correspondent Malcolm Browne, "in the degree of surveillance and control the military has over the correspondents."[8]

Heavy-handed government censorship was only part of the problem confronting U.S. citizens wanting to make informed judgments about the war. They also faced biases in the U.S. media. According to Colman McCarthy, twenty-five of twenty-six major U.S. newspapers supported the Gulf War.[9] The print and other media uncritically adopted Pentagon phrases such as "collateral damage" and "smart bombs." After the war it was reported that only 6,520 of 88,500 tons of bombs dropped on Iraq and Kuwait were "smart," and even these often hit targets that were important to the civilian population. The media throughout the war helped to sanitize civilian casualties and reduced the war to a glorified video game.

A report by *Fairness & Accuracy In Reporting* (FAIR) describes the conflict of interest of major TV news channels that are owned by major corporations tied to military weapons production and oil:

> Most of the corporate-owned media have close relationships to the military and industry: The chair of Capital Cities/ABC . . . is on the board of Texaco, and CBS's board includes directors from Honeywell and the Rand Corporation. But no news outlet is as potentially compromised as NBC, wholly owned by General Electric. . . . In 1989 alone GE received nearly $2 billion in U.S. military contracts for systems employed in the Gulf War effort. . . .

NBC's potential conflicts go beyond weaponry. The government of Kuwait is believed to be a major GE stockholder, having owned 2.1 percent of GE stock in 1982, the last year for which figures are available. . . . Having profited from weapons systems used in the Gulf, and anticipating lucrative deals for restocking U.S. arsenals, GE is also poised to profit from the rebuilding of Kuwait. GE told the *Wall Street Journal* (3/21/91) it expects to win contracts worth "hundreds of millions of dollars."[10]

Conflict of interest may help explain the results of a FAIR survey of sources for ABC, CBS, and NBC nightly news. The survey "found that of 878 on-air sources, only one was a representative of a national peace organization." This, FAIR noted, contrasted with the fact that "seven players from the Super Bowl were brought on to comment on the War."[11]

The role of the U.S. mass media and government censorship in the Gulf War is a frightening illustration of an important aspect of the new world order. In general, the major media served as an uncritical channel of information from the Pentagon to the U.S. people while catering to the emotions and patriotism of a public concerned about the well-being of U.S. troops. Media cooperation with Pentagon news management was so effective it prompted former Reagan administration official Michael Deaver to comment: "If you were going to hire a public relations firm to do the media relations for an international event, it couldn't be done any better than this is being done."[12]

The coverage of the war conveniently ignored critical underlying issues, including the relationship of the Gulf War to the institutional imperatives of the U.S. National Security Establishment. Even before the Gulf War there were disturbing examples of a U.S. National Security Establishment out of control. Each of five examples, which the reader can explore in greater detail through cited sources, illustrates how the U.S. National Security State's propensity for secrecy and covert activities has seriously compromised U.S. democracy.

*The first example of a National Security State crisis is the Iran-Contra affair,* in which proceeds from illegal arms shipments to Iran were diverted to the Nicaraguan Contras during a Congressional ban on such funding. Illegal arms sales and money transfers were only the tip of the iceberg in a disturbing scandal. Segments of the National Security Establishment, with leadership from the White House, the National Security Council, and the head of the Central Intelligence Agency, had taken over many aspects of U.S. foreign policy, subverted the Constitution, and bypassed the U.S. Congress. "My objective all along," former National Security Advisor John Poindexter testified, "was to withhold from the Congress exactly what the [National Security Council] was doing in carrying out the President's policy." Oliver North told Senate Chief Counsel Arthur Liman that CIA director William Casey was setting up "an off-the-shelf, self-sustaining, stand alone entity, that could perform certain activities on behalf of the United States."

This "off-the-shelf" entity, according to the Christic Institute, has been operating in one form or another for twenty-five years. It constitutes a kind of "shadow government," in which "U.S. military and CIA officials, acting both officially and on their own, have waged secret wars, toppled governments, trafficked in drugs, assassinated political enemies, stolen from the U.S. government, and subverted the will of the Constitution, the Congress, and the American people."[13]

It is disconcerting that most of the guilty parties involved in the Iran-Contra scandal were never tried or received little or no punishment for their crimes. Their defense lawyers successfully argued that information vital to their clients' defense could not be made public because it would compromise national security. In other words, the subversion of the Constitution by members of the U.S. National Security State Establishment became relatively risk free because "national security interests" could not be jeopardized. Even more disturbing, in the aftermath of the Iran-Contra scandal the U.S. Congress took steps to increase presidential powers to wage covert wars. Bill Moyers, in a *Frontline* special, "High Crimes and Misdemeanors," underscores the Constitutional crisis inherent in a National Security State:

> What happened in Iran-Contra was nothing less than the systematic disregard for democracy itself. It was, in effect, a coup. . . . Officials who boasted of themselves as men of

the Constitution showed utter contempt for the law. They had the money and power to do what they wanted, the guile to hide their tracks and the arrogance simply to declare what they did was legal. . . . The frightening thing is . . . that it could happen again. . . . The men responsible for Iran-Contra, except a few, have been absolved, exonerated or reprieved. . . . The Government continues to hide its dirty linen behind top secret classifications. . . . With little debate and scant attention from the media, the House and Senate agree on a new intelligence bill giving the President wider power than ever to conduct covert operations using any agency he pleases.[14]

*A second example of a National Security State crisis within the United States is the number of crucial decisions made by presidential directive without Congressional approval or public scrutiny.* President Reagan issued at least 280 secret National Security Decision Directives during his two terms in office.[15] The content of most of these directives remains a mystery to the U.S. people. However, one was leaked and later described by the Christic Institute. In April 1986 President Reagan issued a secret directive that authorized the creation of ten military detention centers within the United States capable of housing 400,000 political prisoners. These detention centers were to be used "in the event that President Reagan chose to [suspend the Constitution and] declare a 'State of Domestic National Emergency' concurrent with the launching of a direct United States military operation into Central America."[16] This example, describing only one of 280 secret National Security Decision Directives, should raise serious questions about what else is being planned in secret and by whom in the name of "national security."

*A third pre-Gulf sign of a U.S. National Security State crisis is the relationship between the international drug trade and U.S. foreign policy.* Elements of the National Security State Establishment from Indochina to Afghanistan to Central America have tolerated and even facilitated the drug trade in exchange for support for U.S. covert operations. "Far from considering drug networks their enemy," Peter Dale Scott and Jonathan Marshall write in *Cocaine Politics: Drugs, Armies and the CIA in Central*

*America*, "U.S. intelligence organizations have made them an essential ally in the covert expansion of American influence abroad."[17]

Senator John Kerry conducted extensive investigations of U.S. foreign policy links to the illegal drug trade. "The narcotics problem," Senator Kerry's report *Drugs, Law, and Foreign Policy* notes, "is a national security and foreign policy issue of significant proportions." He documents how foreign policy considerations predominated so that "each U.S. government agency which had any relationship with Manuel Noriega turned a blind eye to his drug smuggling as he was emerging as a key player on behalf of the Medellín cartel." Kerry also stated that there "was substantial evidence of drug smuggling through the war zones" on the part of the Contras and their supporters. U.S. links to the Contra drug trade included direct "payments to drug traffickers by the U.S. State Department [from] funds authorized by the Congress for humanitarian assistance to the Contras, in some cases after the traffickers had been indicted by federal law enforcement agencies on drug charges." The Kerry report summarizes the relationship between U.S. foreign policy and the drug trade as follows:

> Foreign policy considerations have interfered with the United States' ability to fight the war on drugs. Foreign policy priorities ... halted or interfered with U.S. law enforcement efforts to keep narcotics out of the United States. Within the United States, drug traffickers have manipulated the U.S. judicial system by providing services in support of U.S. foreign policy. U.S. officials involved in Central America failed to address the drug issue for fear of jeopardizing the war effort against Nicaragua.[18]

"I find it useful to think of the whole country as a family system that has this dirty secret that we're ashamed to admit," says Father Bill Teska, an Episcopalian priest who has worked to expose the relationship of U.S. foreign policy and drugs. "Our government has actually cooperated with drug dealers and has assisted in the importation of drugs into this country when it suited its purposes . . . such as national security or overthrowing the government of Nicaragua."[19]

*A fourth example that gives credence to concerns about a National Security State taking hold in U.S. society is related to charges of impropriety during the 1980 U.S. presidential election.* According to Gary Sick, a member of the Carter administration's National Security Council, there is substantial evidence suggesting that the Reagan-Bush team arranged to keep the hostages in Iran until after the 1980 election in exchange for future arms shipments to Iran. The inability to free the hostages insured the electoral defeat of a beleaguered Jimmy Carter. "The hostages were released on January 21, 1981," Gary Sick writes, "within minutes after Reagan was sworn in as president. Almost immediately thereafter . . . arms began to flow to Iran in substantial quantities."[20] Former Iranian President Bani-Sadr, in his book *My Turn to Speak: Iran, the Revolution and Secret Deals with the U.S.,* verifies that a deal was made. The "sole purpose" of negotiations between the Reagan campaign and Iran "was to handicap Carter's reelection bid by preventing the hostages' release" before the November election.[21] It was announced in August 1991 that Congress planned to investigate these charges of impropriety during the 1980 election.

*A fifth sign of a U.S. National Security State crisis is a 1987 meeting of the Conference of American Armies held in Argentina.* The meeting brought together military commanders from Argentina, Uruguay, Chile, Paraguay, Bolivia, Brazil, Peru, Ecuador, Colombia, Venezuela, Panama, Honduras, Guatemala, El Salvador, *and the United States.* The conference focused on the threat that liberation theology and the progressive churches posed to the national security of the Americas. It linked liberation theology to an international communist conspiracy and called for a strategy of continental security measures, which included the coordination of military intelligence and operations. The conference report specifically named Ignacio Ellacuría, a Jesuit priest who directed the Catholic University in El Salvador until his brutal murder in November 1989, as a person who consciously manipulated "the truly liberating Christian message of salvation to further the objectives of the Communist revolution."[22] Such language in the context of

National Security States is a license to kill. According to an article in the *National Catholic Reporter* the generals, in addition to targeting liberation theology as an enemy, also supported use of elections as a cover for their own de facto rule. The generals, apparently including U.S. participants, indicated that they opposed a new wave of military coups throughout the Americas, preferring instead *"a permanent state of military control over civilian government, while still preserving formal democracy."* [Emphasis added.][23]

## Conclusion

The United States, like El Salvador, demonstrates many features of a National Security State. Democracy in both countries is now seriously compromised by the powers vested in the military and broader National Security Establishment. In the United States this establishment includes the military-industrial complex and institutions such as the National Security Council and the Central Intelligence Agency. It is largely unaccountable to the U.S. people.

The five examples of a National Security State crisis discussed above collectively add weight to my thesis that behind the Gulf War and the so-called new world order are the priorities of the National Security Establishment. President Eisenhower's warning of "the disastrous rise of misplaced power" is truly prophetic in the context of the Gulf crisis. The end of the Cold War, as the next two chapters illustrate, offered the possibility of U.S. economic renewal but not without reordering priorities away from the military sector. As in El Salvador, the U.S. National Security Establishment fought to preserve its institutional privileges. It was well-positioned to do so after forty years of growing influence within U.S. society.

The quotation from the Washington Office on Latin America which I used earlier to describe the Salvadoran military's hostility to a negotiated settlement of El Salvador's civil war is reprinted below. It captures well a similar dynamic operating within the U.S. National Security Establishment as it confronted the dangerous prospect of institutional decline in light of the end of the Cold War:

Despite the presence of some moderate officers ... successful pursuit of a negotiated settlement would directly threaten the interests of individual officers as well as those of their institution.... Within the officer corps ... the arguments against negotiations remain persuasive: First, any reduction in troop size as a result of negotiations would necessitate a corresponding reduction in the officer corps.... Second, as the Armed Forces have expanded in size and wealth because of the war, so too has their influence. By any estimate, the military stands as the country's single most powerful social and economic institution. ... Consequently, any progress toward a negotiated settlement would challenge the military's privileged position within the government and society.

The imperatives of a National Security State are the hidden dynamics behind the Gulf War and the new world order. The U.S. National Security Establishment used the Gulf crisis to foreclose on the peace dividend, to block economic renewal, and to shape a world order in which U.S. superpower status is guaranteed through military power.

CHAPTER 5

# Policing the Brave New World Order

*The end of the Cold War has been a victory for all humanity.*
—President George Bush
State of the Union Address, January 29, 1991

*It seemed to many Americans that the end of the Cold War was a God-send for the United States, an opportunity to gather our energies and prepare for the new challenges of the twenty-first century. While this would appear to be the preferred outcome of the Cold War I fear that the actual outcome will be rather different and far less attractive. . . . The Cold War system that has dominated our lives for so long will be replaced, not with a new system of international peace and stability, but with a new war system of interminable conflict between the industrialized countries of the North and the underdeveloped forces and nations of the South. . . . While such conflicts may not appear to have the connected, coherent character of the struggle between East and West they nevertheless add up to an ongoing systemic and global struggle for wealth and power. . . . Unless things change radically in the months and years ahead I believe that this struggle between North and South will come to dominate American life and society every bit as powerfully and pervasively as did the global struggle between East and West. It will also erase all the benefits that might have come at the end of the Cold War.*
—Michael Klare
Director of Peace and World Security Studies
Hampshire College, October 8, 1990

55

A few years ago at a high school outside of Minneapolis a retired military officer ended his speech by pounding his fists on the podium, saying: "We must be forever vigilant against the threat of world peace." His comment, perhaps a slip of the tongue, provides an accurate summary of how the U.S. National Security Establishment viewed the end of the Cold War.

The Cold War thaw led to a national crisis involving a struggle over power and identity. The war with Iraq and the present shape of the "new world order" reflect the outcome of this power struggle. The "Soviet threat" was the glue that held U.S. society together. It fed a national mythology of the United States as a "benevolent superpower" up against the "evil empire"; it justified the maintenance of more than 375 U.S. foreign military bases and the deployment of more than half a million U.S. troops (before the Gulf War) on foreign soil;[1] it provided ideological cover for the use of these troops and bases to support more than 200 U.S. military interventions in the Third World;[2] it led to enormous wealth and power for the military-industrial complex and the managers of the U.S. National Security Establishment; and, it diffused internal tensions in a society divided between rich and poor by focusing attention on a "common enemy." For all of these reasons *the end of the Cold War led to a national identity crisis reflected in an unprecedented internal power struggle over the future of the nation.*

Senator David Boren, Chairman of the Senate Intelligence Committee, told the National Press Club in April, 1990:

> In one way we have had a strange and symbiotic relationship with the Soviet Union. It may sound like an odd thing to say but I don't think we fully understand the implications of the decline of the Soviet Union for the United States. It could very well lead to our decline as well. . . . The European countries and Japan have been willing to follow our lead over the past decades because they needed us. As long as there was an external Soviet threat . . . and we were providing the shield of protection then they needed the United States and so they were following our lead. But what about now in these changing circumstances? Are they going to continue to follow our lead in

the future now that they no longer need us as a shield? I don't think so.[3]

## Military or Economic Strength: A Choice

The end of the Cold War was indeed a time of peril and opportunity for the United States. In the "new" order taking shape it seemed that superpower military confrontation was giving way to economic competition among the dominant powers. The United States could not maintain a costly, global military network *and* economically compete with Western Europe and Japan.

James Petras describes a "deep-rooted sense of decline and fear of growing challenges to [U.S.] global supremacy":

Prior to the Gulf War there were numerous indications that the global decline of the United States was accelerating. In Eastern Europe and the Soviet Union the "ideological victory" over Stalinism also revealed the tremendous incapacity of the United States to provide economic resources to reshape these economies to its needs or even to subsidize new client regimes. Instead, most observers saw Germany as the dominant power. . . . At the policy level, declining influence became obvious in Washington's incapacity to impose its liberal agricultural and "services" . . . agenda. . . . The cumulative gains of Japan and its virtual displacement of the United States as the major investor and trading partner in Asia . . . are a clear signal of declining influence. In a world in which global power is increasingly determined by industrial and financial activities and market exchanges based on strong industrial states, Washington strategists must have recognized that the United States will be a sure loser. The decline of U.S. global power is evident even in Latin America. . . . Bush's "Enterprise for the Americas" proposal was more rhetoric than substance, more pillage of existing markets and resources than any strategic commitment to large-scale long-term investments to expand productive capacity. The initial sums promised ($300 million) would cover Latin

America's foreign debt payments for four days. More to the point, the continuing massive outflows of interest payments and profits from Latin America to the United States ($35 billion per year) and the incapacity of the United States to reconstruct the economies of small, reconquered nations (Grenada, Panama, Nicaragua) demonstrate the tremendous gap between U.S. power to dominate and U.S. incapacity to rebuild economically viable client states.[4]

Economic revitalization would be difficult for the United States under the best of circumstances. The problems described in Chapter 2, including poverty, homelessness, eroded infrastructure, the lack of productive investment, the waste of human capital reflected in expanded prisons and inadequate health and education systems, and huge budget and trade deficits all point to economic crisis and decline. These problems are aggravated by decades of huge military expenditures and the absence of any serious government or industry planning for "peace conversion," the process whereby military industries convert to socially useful production.

Senator Boren was among a number of U.S. leaders who prior to the Gulf War argued that critical choices between "guns" and "butter" could no longer be avoided. The United States could not hope to revitalize its economy if the military maintained its dominant role and if more than eighty percent of U.S. federally funded research and development dollars continued to serve military priorities. Other analysts agreed. "The United States," wrote Theodore Sorenson in a pre-Gulf crisis article entitled "Rethinking National Security," "cannot modernize its industrial base, cannot devote the necessary resources to the revitalization of the economy, if we persist in the folly of continuing to devote federal funds for research and development almost exclusively to military and space uses."[5]

There were two distinct choices confronting the United States as the Cold War ended. The country had come to a fork in a road. One path stressed the importance of economic revitalization and the need to redirect resources away from the military. The other path stressed U.S. military power as the means to maintain U.S. superpower status. It had to choose.

## The "Threat of Peace"

Some U.S. leaders understood that economic power would ultimately determine leadership and status in the emerging world order and that U.S. economic well-being required a shift away from military priorities. However, Michael Klare notes, the idea of a shift from military to economic competition was "a terrifying prospect for ... those leaders who for so long have directed the National Security Establishment. ... For these leaders whose identity is so closely tied up with being number one, the loss of our paramount status as a superpower is an unacceptable prospect."[6]

For years the power and privilege of the U.S. military and National Security Establishment were directly linked to the Soviet threat. It was the Cold War that fed institutional interests and personal ambition and prestige. The prospect, or inflated prospect, of a conventional or nuclear confrontation in Europe was used to justify huge military expenditures and expensive weapons systems. Approximately $150 billion of each year's military budget was directly or indirectly related to the defense of Western Europe.

In 1987, when U.S. and Soviet negotiators came to an agreement on details of the INF (Intermediate-range Nuclear Forces) treaty, the *Spokane Chronicle*'s headline read, "Peace may not be best for Boeing; upcoming (INF) treaty may lead to cuts in defense budget." The *Defense News* warned at the same time that "defense related stock-trading values have fallen so precipitously in the past two weeks that one Wall Street analyst says investors appear to be reacting to the 'fear of an outbreak of world peace.' "[7]

The end of the Cold War was a far more serious threat to the military industrial complex than the INF treaty. The December 1989 issue of *National Defense: Journal of the American Defense Preparedness Association* warned that cuts in military spending would result in cancellations of major weapons systems. The industry, however, was going to fight to "hold the line" on such cutbacks, especially on weapons systems already in development. The news was not all bad, the journal reported, because "the coming Decade of Uncertainty will be a time of unprecedented opportunity for Special Operations Forces (SOF) and Low-Intensity Warfare (LIW)."[8]

Defense industry journals and military service reports in the aftermath of the Cold War reflected a palpable sense of anxiety, even panic. The Cold War thaw offered the possibility that many billions of dollars could be shifted from the military to other purposes. A substantial peace dividend seemed likely in light of U.S. poverty and economic decline. As a result, there was a desperate search among the various military branches and weapons producers for institutional legitimacy and for an ongoing role in a world order that had unexpectedly changed. A section of the May 1990 issue of the *Marine Corps Gazette* entitled "On the Corps' Continuing Role" illustrates these dynamics. It says in part:

> The world is "in the midst of historic and promising transformations in the global security environment," experiencing changes more sweeping than any since the outbreak of World War II. . . . That the Cold War is over and the threat of global conflict has greatly diminished are widely held perceptions. Hopes for a "peace dividend" continue to be voiced, and major cutbacks in defense expenditures are regarded as virtual certainties.
>
> Changes of this magnitude bring periods of "agonizing reappraisal." Clearly, the United States is entering a new era of reexamination of its defense needs. Policy, strategy, Service roles and functions, force structure, weapons systems, and budget levels all come under serious review. . . . The purpose of this section is to help put this challenging period in perspective and to encourage thinking about the Corps' future . . . [to] detail the specific capabilities that Marine Corps forces possess across the spectrum of warfare . . . [and to consider different] approaches the Corps might consider as it comes to grips with harsh budget realities.[9]

The mood of this and other publications and reports was somber but realistic. "Widely held perceptions" of reduced global conflict made a peace dividend almost inevitable. This prompted among the branches of the military a strategy of damage control. First, the size of the "peace dividend" could be limited by finding new enemies and inflating the dangers of old enemies, such as drugs and terrorism, to replace the Soviet threat. Second, the focus of the conflict could be shifted from East/West to North/South, emphasizing the instability of the third-world nations as a threat to our national security. Third, despite earlier reluctance the strategy of low-intensity conflict could be exploited. Each branch of the military and each company, for that matter, hoped to demonstrate that it had unique capabilities for dealing with these new issues of "national security," thus shifting the cost of any peace dividend to others while maintaining its piece of the budget pie.

## The Search for Enemies

The post–Cold War search for enemies began immediately. U.S. military branches that had expressed reluctance about U.S. military involvement in "drug wars" suddenly began citing "narco-terrorism" as a serious threat to U.S. national security. General A. M. Gray, Commandant of the Marine Corps, in March, 1990, warned Congress about "narcoterrorism" and stated that "drug use and trafficking will continue to undermine both international and domestic stability."[10] The next month the U.S. Army Chief of Staff, Carl E. Vuono, highlighted "the scourge of drugs" as a threat to U.S. national security.[11]

The "war on drugs" is particularly suspect as a stand-in for the Soviet threat. "The only thing we know with certainty," according to Michael Levine, a former Drug Enforcement Agency (DEA) undercover agent, "is that the Drug War is not for real. The drug economy in the United States is as much as $200 billion a year, and it is being used to finance political operations."[12] U.S. foreign policy uses the so-called drug war as a cover to expand greatly its military presence in Latin America and, as I described in the previous chapter, there are friendly ties between U.S. covert operations and international drug traffickers.

It also is futile, as past efforts have shown, to use military force to attempt to stop the drug flow at the source without addressing the economic realities of hundreds of thousands of poor campesinos who depend on such production for survival. The use of force on the consumer end is equally problematic. A police and prison approach to drugs within the United States takes funds away from much-needed treatment centers, targets the poor rather than a much larger group of affluent users, ignores the social conditions that make drug trafficking attractive to many youth suffocating in inner cities, leaves the bankers and other elite economic sectors that garner most of the drug profits largely untouched, puts police in constant danger, leads to greater violence in neighborhoods, and threatens to erode civil liberties.

In short, the drug war is a failure in terms of stated objectives. However, it serves two important functions for the military and broader National Security Establishment. It is a convenient cover for a greatly expanded U.S. military presence in Latin America, and it helps hold off the threat of a peace dividend.

Drug-related threats to national security are not the only enemies called on to replace the Soviet threat. There is also the ongoing specter of terrorism. General Gray warned that "nationalism and terrorism are on the rise." Terrorism, he said, "will continue to be the preferred means for radical nations and groups to achieve their ends since it is an inexpensive means of warfare."[13]

## Shift of Focus to the Third World

Newfound enemies which focused on drugs and terrorism were part of a broader effort in the post–Cold War environment to transfer national security concerns from Europe to the Third World. "Our national interests no longer are focused primarily on east to west," General Gray told Congress, "but have evolved to include north and south."[14] General Carl E. Vuono, U.S. Army Chief of Staff, also stressed the preoccupation with third-world enemies:

Because the United States is a global power with vital interests that must be protected throughout an increasingly turbulent world, we must look beyond the European continent and consider other threats to our security. The proliferation of military power in what is called the "Third World" presents a troubling picture. . . . The growing challenge of insurgencies, subversion, international terrorism, and the scourge of drugs—often grouped under the term "low-intensity conflict"—constitutes yet another serious threat to our interests. . . . As a global power with economic, political, and security interests spanning the world, the United States cannot ignore those political threats to those interests.[15]

The geographic and ideological shift in enemies from the Soviet Union to the Third World and from an East-West to a North-South conflict is justified by the military on economic grounds. Poverty-induced social turmoil, according to General Gray, threatens U.S. access to vital raw materials and resources located throughout the Third World:

The underdeveloped world's growing dissatisfaction over the gap between rich and poor nations will create a fertile breeding ground for insurgencies. These insurgencies have the potential to jeopardize regional stability and our access to vital economic and military resources. This situation will become critical as our Nation and allies and potential adversaries become more and more dependent on these strategic resources. If we are to have stability in these regions, maintain access to their resources, protect our citizens abroad, defend our vital installations, and deter conflict, we must maintain within our active force structure a credible military power projection capability with the flexibility to respond to conflict across the spectrum of violence throughout the globe.[16]

General Maxwell Taylor had warned years before that "as the leading 'have' power" the United States "may expect to fight to protect our national valuables against envious 'have nots.' "[17] The U.S. war against the poor, according to General Gray and other U.S. military leaders, would take on greater urgency in the post–Cold War period where inequalities would be more pronounced:

> In many regions, poverty has become institutionalized with little hope of relief. Within the next 20 years, the earth's population will be approximately 150 percent of today's level. Eighty percent of this population will reside in the developing nations of Asia, Africa, and Latin America. . . . Competition for limited resources, such as food, water, and housing, will continue to make these regions breeding grounds of discontent. Already, insurgencies are ongoing in the Pacific, Latin America, and Africa. Their numbers will increase, perhaps dramatically, in the short term.[18]

Thus U.S. military leaders were taking aim at the peace dividend by challenging critics who believed that there was a conflict between superpower military and superpower economic status. A shift away from U.S. military priorities, according to General Gray, would not lead to economic revitalization but to economic vulnerability, because U.S. military power guarantees U.S. businesses access to raw materials and markets:

> Our superpower political and military status is dependent upon our ability to maintain the economic base derived from our ability to compete in established and developing economic markets throughout the world. If we are to maintain this status, we must have unimpeded access to these markets and to the resources needed to support our manufacturing requirements. In addition, our ability to operate successfully and confidently within these markets and to protect our citizens abroad is dependent on the stability of the regions in which they are located.[19]

That is, in the post–Cold War world U.S. economic well-being will depend on the effectiveness of the U.S. military. General Gray countered the economic revitalization issue in another way as well. In contrast to those who emphasized the folly of trying to compete with Western Europe and Japan while gearing research and development to the military sector he stressed the importance of the military sector and emphasized its utility to the civilian economy:

> Many of the technologies that will be applied to the battlefield of the next century have already been identified. Directed energy and laser weaponry, improved sensors, robotics, stealth, and superior space systems are already being developed. Genetic engineering and other biotechnologies will lead to capabilities in chemical and biological weaponry never before envisioned. ... If our Nation is to maintain military credibility in the next century, we must continue to exploit affordable new technology. Fiscal restraints and responsibility will require that the development and exploitation of technology have both civilian and military applicability.[20]

The military's constant theme in these documents is that although the Cold War has reduced U.S.-Soviet tensions the United States is a nation under attack in a turbulent and hostile world. A peace dividend is not only shortsighted, but it may be fatal to the nation's security. "Economic and political instability threatens nations in all regions of the world," General Gray told Congress. "Conflict of some type in each of these regions is ongoing and likely to continue. If we are to maintain our position as a world leader and protect our interests, we must be capable of and willing to protect our global interests. This requires that we maintain our capability to respond to likely regions of conflict."[21]

The arguments advanced by the military and defense establishment are flawed and self-serving to say the least. Social turmoil and instability are consequences of poverty and social inequality within and among nations. However, to seek to resolve these conflicts through military power, and without a measure of economic justice, is both fruitless and dangerous. If the United States chooses a path of economic justice it can reduce social tensions and gain access to necessary resources by purchasing them. If it forsakes economic justice social turmoil will undoubtedly increase. However, third-world countries need to sell their resources and the policing function of the IMF ensures that they do so.

## New Support for Low-Intensity Conflict

Along with the search for new enemies to replace the Soviet threat after the Cold War, the U.S. military suddenly reversed itself and became an enthusiastic supporter of low-intensity conflict (LIC), a Pentagon term which describes threats to U.S. interests in third-world countries that are less violent than conventional or nuclear wars. LIC also refers to the U.S. strategy of protecting perceived interests in light of such threats. According to one definition from the Joint Chiefs of Staff, LIC is a "limited politico-military struggle to achieve political, social, economic, or psychological objectives. It is often protracted and ranges from diplomatic, economic, and psychosocial pressures through terrorism and insurgency."[22]

A detailed analysis of low-intensity conflict is available elsewhere. The key point to be made here is that *until after the Cold War the U.S. military was a reluctant partner in LIC.* LIC required the military to develop nontraditional weapons and strategies that were seen as a threat to high-technology systems on which their huge budgets and prestige depends. Pentagon consultant Noel Koch argued that the U.S. military needed significant reorientation in the aftermath of the Vietnam war. However, according to Koch, such "a development has been strenuously resisted, and this resistance has been centered in the U.S. military."[23] The military's resistance was a practical one: it associated low-intensity conflict with low budgets.

Although LIC played an important role in U.S. interventions throughout the 1980s, U.S. military leaders clearly considered it a sideshow in which the main attraction was the Soviet threat. The Cold War was their ticket to huge budgets and high-tech weapons systems. The U.S. military in the post–Cold War period suddenly shifted its rhetoric from a reluctant partner to an enthusiastic supporter of low-intensity conflict. This was true because LIC, like drugs and terrorism, was one of the few games left in town.

Present day low-intensity-conflict strategy is a response to military and political failures that led to the defeat of the United States in Indochina, a setting where the highly technological conventional and nuclear weapons preferred by the U.S. military were inappropriate. The U.S. military, which profited handsomely from sophisticated weapons systems, believed that sufficient conventional firepower combined with the threat of nuclear bombs would win wars. Not only did the United States lack quick strike, highly mobile, special operations forces (SOFs) capable of fighting guerrilla wars, it also lacked a comprehensive strategy to control both territory and "hearts and minds."

As stated above, U.S. foreign policy in the 1980s, despite resistance from important sectors of the U.S. military, assigned a significant role to LIC as a means to better intervene in third-world countries. The United States greatly improved its special operations forces and developed a sophisticated strategy for third-world interventionism that integrated political-diplomatic, military, economic, and psychological aspects of warfare. It was a deadly means of warfare against the organized poor in Central America and other third-world countries where perceived U.S. interests were threatened.[24]

U.S. low-intensity-conflict strategy has also been shaped by political considerations. The death of more than fifty thousand U.S. soldiers in a protracted ground war in a far-off country had serious political fallout. It resulted in what came to be called the Vietnam Syndrome, the reluctance of U.S. citizens in the post-Vietnam era to support the defense of "vital" interests overseas through the projection of U.S. power, including deployment of U.S. troops. This syndrome, lamentable from the point of view of the U.S. economic and military elites, was one target of the Gulf War.

The Vietnam Syndrome shapes U.S. low-intensity-conflict strategy in a variety of ways. LIC emphasizes U.S. training and support for surrogate forces, such as the Nicaraguan Contras or Salvadoran military. These groups are a throwback to an earlier time in U.S. history when the wealthy could hire replacement soldiers for their sons. In its present form surrogate forces are funded and trained to do the dying on behalf of U.S. national security interests. This racist strategy allows many thousands of third-world people to die with minimal U.S. public protest because it reduces the number of U.S. casualties. LIC also limits public awareness, concern, and debate through its use of disinformation campaigns and covert operations.[25]

U.S. conduct in the Gulf War reflects key features of LIC even though the war with Iraq could not be considered a low-intensity conflict. Common elements in U.S. LIC strategy in Central America and U.S. strategy in the Gulf include the following:

• U.S. warfare strategy in both regions was shaped by the Vietnam Syndrome. In Central America surrogate troops replaced U.S. casualties in defense of "vital security interests." In Iraq the same result was achieved through the largest aerial bombings in human history. U.S. policy makers in both regions acted with confidence, unfortunately borne out by events, that the U.S. people would tolerate the mass slaughter of others as long as U.S. casualties were light. According to Bob Woodward's book *The Commanders*, General Colin Powell, head of the Joint Chiefs of Staff, was more reluctant than President Bush to seek a military solution to the Gulf crisis because of fears of the negative political fallout for the U.S. military if U.S. casualties were unacceptably high.[26]

• The U.S. government, in order to garner support for highly questionable policies in Central America and the Gulf, targeted the U.S. people with disinformation and propaganda.

• A major purpose of U.S.-sponsored wars in both regions was intimidation through mass destruction. CIA director William Casey boasted that U.S. sponsorship of the Contras in Nicaragua was intended to "waste" the country.[27] Richard John Neuhaus, a supporter of the U.S. war against Nicaragua, stated, "Washington believes that Nicaragua must serve as a warning to the rest of Central America to never again challenge U.S. hegemony because of the enormous economic and political costs. It's too bad that the poor have to suffer, but historically the poor have always suffered. Nicaragua must be a lesson to the others."[28] Iraq provided a similar lesson in the aftermath of the Cold War. The U.S. demonstrated that it was the lone military superpower, willing to flex its military muscles, and unwilling to tolerate disobedience.

• The Central American and Gulf Wars were fought to maintain control over governments in areas considered strategic to the United States.

- U.S. policies in both regions stressed military "solutions" over diplomacy.
- Finally, U.S. backing for the rich against the poor was a significant factor in both the Central American and Gulf Wars.

Clearly the principles of low-intensity conflict have taken hold, providing the National Security Establishment with partial "solutions" to the problems posed by the peace dividend and the Vietnam Syndrome. The military, while not limiting itself to low-intensity conflicts, is eager to exploit the possibilities of LIC in the post–Cold War period. General Carl E. Vuono, in a 1990 report entitled *Trained and Ready in an Era of Change*, indicated that "LIC is the security challenge most likely to confront the Army in the 1990s."[29] General Gray of the Marine Corps also jumped on the low-intensity conflict bandwagon. He stated that the majority of the conflicts confronting the United States in the future "would be at the low- to mid-intensity level of conflict."[30] Michael Klare has pointed out that in the post–Cold War, pre–Gulf War period, despite their earlier reservations, "all four of the military services have asserted recently that they are *uniquely* suited to perform the LIC function."[31]

## Conclusion

In the post–Cold War period the United States faced a hidden struggle that would determine the viability of its democracy. A peace dividend and new world order based on nonmilitary forms of conflict resolution threatened powerful interests. The military was seeking to create a world in its own image. It placed at the center of this world its own institutional privileges and those of the broader National Security State Establishment. If the National Security Establishment had its way, economic revitalization would give way to militarism. What it needed was a crisis to make all this talk of post–Cold War enemies plausible.

General Gray warned that due to the "proliferation of sophisticated weapons" there were areas where low-intensity conflict might not succeed and greater violence would be needed:

Throughout the world, the proliferation of arms is increasing at a dangerous pace. The variety of weapons systems available and their lethality has dramatically increased. The range of weapons technology encompasses nuclear weapons, chemical weapons, ballistic missile technology, sophisticated aircraft, submarines, armor, armored vehicles, and precision guided munitions.[32]

The advanced weapons systems designed to "defend" Europe could in the post–Cold War period be used against well-armed third-world enemies. Of particular concern was the Middle East where "social dissatisfaction with Western secular ideas continues to provide a breeding ground for terrorism and instability."[33] "In the Middle East," General Gray stated, "it will remain in our interest to maintain stability for both economic and political reasons since many of our allies depend on the region for the majority of their oil supply."[34]

If the end of the Cold War was, in the words of Michael Klare, a "God-send" to a nation in economic crisis and in desperate need of a peace dividend, then the Gulf crisis demonstrated that there is another more powerful god in charge: the god of the National Security State.

CHAPTER 6

# The Gulf War and

# the Brave New World Order

*On present form, the much-vaunted new world order will be indistinguishable from a pax Americana. . . . In the end, military and political power depend on economic power. The pax Britannica of the 19th century was built on the industrial supremacy of Lancashire and the financial supremacy of the City of London at least as much as on the guns of the Royal Navy. Present-day Americans have no such assets. In the business of wealth creation they are almost as outclassed as we [Britons] are. . . . Unfortunately a bankrupt world policeman, haunted by the sense of economic failure and anxious to compensate for it, may well be more dangerous than a rich and confident one.*

— Daniel Marquand, *Manchester Guardian Weekly*

*It was a time of great and exalting excitement. The country was up in arms, the war was on, in every breast burned the holy fire of patriotism; the drums were beating, the bands were playing, the toy pistols popping, the bunched firecrackers hissing and spluttering; on every hand and far down the receding and fading spread of roofs and balconies a fluttering of flags flashed in the sun.*

— Mark Twain, *The War Prayer*

The Commandant of the Marine Corps told Congress in March 1990 that "the people of our great Nation continue to demand that we maintain our status as a superpower."[1] In fact, through the Gulf crisis the U.S. military and broader National Security Establishment took steps to ensure that the United States would shape a new world order in which the principal U.S. role is that of a *military* superpower. Michael Klare captured the underlying issues in a talk at the University of Minnesota in October 1990.

> Something else is also at work here [in the Persian Gulf], something more visceral . . . than the protection merely of vital interests. I believe that many American leaders are motivated by a psychological need to preserve America's role as a global superpower in the post Cold War era, and to retain thereby their power and prestige as the managers of the National Security Establishment. This preoccupation with . . . global dominance emerges out of the changing global landscape and the crisis in American leadership brought about by the end of the Cold War. For years Americans reveled in our status as the leaders of the so-called free world even if it meant squandering our wealth on military forces while Japan and Germany devoted their wealth to economic primacy. But with the end of the Cold War our claim to superpower status is put in jeopardy.[2]

The U.S. National Security Establishment, with leadership from President Bush, orchestrated the Gulf crisis. It was a ticket to remaining a superpower and shaping a new world order in which military power mattered more than the economic health of the country.

## Opportunity Lost

The end of the Cold War offered the possibility for U.S. economic revitalization and for a world order in which conflicts could be resolved through negotiations rather than violence. The Gulf War closed the door on these new possibilities. There is substantial circumstantial evidence to suggest that the United States encouraged Saddam Hussein's plans to invade Kuwait. The U.S. ambassador to Iraq, April Glaspie, assured Saddam

Hussein eight days before the invasion that the U.S. policy was to maintain neutrality in its border dispute with Kuwait. "We have no opinion on the Arab-Arab conflicts, like your border disagreement with Kuwait," Glaspie told Hussein. "James Baker has directed our official spokesmen to emphasize this instruction."[3] Assistant Secretary of State for Near Eastern Affairs John Kelly told Congress two days before the invasion that despite reports by U.S. intelligence sources of an imminent Iraqi attack the U.S. had no intention to defend Kuwait.[4]

Whether or not Saddam Hussein invaded Kuwait with false assurances from the U.S. government makes for interesting debate, but it doesn't change the fundamental issue. The U.S. National Security Establishment manipulated the Gulf crisis in order to defend its institutional privileges. The peace dividend and the possibility of an authentically new international order were intentional casualties of the war.

Immediately after the Iraqi invasion of Kuwait it appeared that without U.S. interference a solution was imminent. In the January 7, 1991, issue of the *New Yorker* Milton Viorst details how the Iraqi invasion of Kuwait was a "last minute decision, made in anger at the Kuwaiti intransigence" during negotiations over a variety of issues of vital concern to Iraq. These issues included access to the Persian Gulf, a disputed oil field, oil prices, and debt:

• The colonial powers had cynically denied Iraq access to the sea when drawing up borders in the region. Iraq wanted control of two uninhabited islands under Kuwaiti jurisdiction.

• The dispute over the Rumalia oil field centered on Iraqi claims that Kuwait was stealing oil by drilling a disproportionate share of oil from fields that lie almost entirely in Iraq.

• Perhaps most infuriating to the Iraqis was the issue of its "debt" to Kuwait. Kuwait helped finance Iraq during the war with Iran. Kuwait provided the dollars, while Iraq provided the bodies in the struggle against a common enemy. After the war Kuwait demanded repayment of these "loans."

• Finally, Iraq accused Kuwait of violating production quotas and thereby conspiring with the United States to keep oil prices artificially low. It was bitterly ironic to the Iraqis that Kuwait was demanding cash at the same time it took steps to reduce Iraq's oil revenues.

Viorst says that both King Fahd of Saudi Arabia and King Hussein of Jordan received assurances from Saddam Hussein within hours of the invasion that "having invaded Kuwait to teach it a lesson, [Iraq] planned to withdraw over the weekend."

> [Upon hearing of the invasion Saudi King] Fahd did not at that time ask for a total Iraqi withdrawal. Instead, he proposed what seemed like a compromise: that the Iraqis withdraw to the disputed border area — a move that would have left them in possession of the Rumalia oil fields and the two islands [which would give Iraq access to the Gulf]. ... What was clear was that he did not at that time express any fear that Saddam Hussein would order his troops to Saudi Arabia.

The crisis, as Viorst documents, seemed well on the way to being resolved only hours after its inception. Friday, August 3, the day after the invasion, Saddam Hussein agreed to attend on Sunday a "limited Arab" summit with the Emir of Kuwait, and leaders from Saudi Arabia, Egypt, Jordan and Yemen, to resolve the crisis. He cautioned, however, "that any public condemnation or threat to Iraq ... would complicate the execution of his withdrawal plan, since withdrawal under those circumstances would convey the impression that he was caving in to pressure."

The "limited Arab summit" fell apart before it happened. Kuwait received approval from the U.N. National Security Council calling for Iraqi withdrawal, the United States warned Saudi Arabia of Iraqi troop movements toward its border, the United States froze Iraqi assets and announced the dispatch of U.S. warships to the Gulf, and Egyptian President Mubarek, under what he described as "tremendous pressure" from the United States, condemned the invasion. On Sunday, the day the "limited summit" was to have resolved the crisis, President Bush held a press conference at which he referred to the Iraqis as "international outlaws and renegades." The vilification of Saddam Hussein had begun.

Having sabotaged initial prospects for an Arab-led negotiated settlement, the United States took what appeared to be promising action: It worked to organize an international coalition capable of applying economic sanctions against Iraq. There are two keys to effective sanctions. First, they must seriously curtail imports and exports to and from the targeted country. Second, they must be linked to negotiations. Economic sanctions were highly successful according to the first yardstick. The CIA estimated that as of December 1990 the sanctions cut off over ninety percent of Iraq's imports and ninety-seven percent of its exports. "Many industries," the CIA indicated, "have largely shut down. Most importantly, the blockade had eliminated any hope Baghdad had of cashing in on higher oil prices or its seizure of Kuwaiti oil fields."[5] Unfortunately, the United States had no intention of linking successful economic sanctions to negotiations; it wanted a military solution in the Gulf.

The economic sanctions throughout the crisis were linked to a U.S. strategy of issuing ultimatums rather than promoting negotiations. Prior to the actual crisis, in the spring of 1990, Saddam Hussein had proposed the elimination of all chemical and nuclear weapons in the Middle East. The United States responded that it was a good idea for Iraq to eliminate such weapons, but it would not encourage other nations in the region, including Israel, to follow suit. Negotiations, backed up by effective economic sanctions, could have permitted discussion of Iraqi grievances against Kuwait while insisting on Iraqi withdrawal. Ultimatums precluded such possibilities. Negotiations backed by sanctions could have led to Iraqi withdrawal while laying a foundation for addressing broader questions in the Middle East, such as the illegal Israeli occupation of Palestine, the problem of weapons states (the by-product of decades of U.S. policy based on establishing regional power brokers to defend U.S. interests), and the need for regional disarmament. Ultimatums closed off such possibilities.

Economic sanctions linked to ultimatums rather than negotiations inevitably led to military confrontation. This was the intent of U.S. policy all along. The United States took unilateral military actions, including the sending of several hundred thousand U.S. troops to the Middle East, at the same time it formed an international coalition around economic sanctions. The U.S.

justified its military actions on the grounds that they were necessary for the defense of Saudi Arabia. President Bush claimed
on September 11 in a joint session to Congress that "within three
days [of the Iraqi invasion], 120,000 Iraqi troops with 850 tanks
had poured into Kuwait and moved south to threaten Saudi
Arabia." However, Jean Heller in a detailed article in the *St.
Petersburg Times* noted that "Soviet satellite photos of Kuwait
taken five weeks after the Iraqi invasion suggest the Bush administration might have exaggerated the scope of Iraq's military
threat to Saudi Arabia at the time." "The Pentagon kept saying
the bad guys were there," Peter Zimmermann, who served with
the U.S. Arms Control and Disarmament Agency during the
Reagan administration, was quoted as saying, "but we don't see
anything to indicate an Iraqi force in Kuwait of even 20 percent
the size the administration claimed."[6]

According to investigative writers Andrew and Leslie Cockburn:

> The initial justification for sending troops to the desert was
> that Saddam was poised to attack Saudi Arabia itself.
> However, CIA officials have privately conceded that at no
> time was there any evidence that Saddam contemplated
> such a move. That was not the news given to the Saudi
> King Fahd by the administration when his permission was
> sought for the military buildup. Fahd was reportedly con-
> vinced by intelligence handed to him by Defense Secretary
> Cheney that his realm was in mortal danger from Saddam's
> tanks.[7]

The United States consistently ignored negotiated solutions
while inflating the crisis and exaggerating the threat posed by
Saddam Hussein. Although Iraq had legitimate grievances
against Kuwait, there was a broad consensus about the character
of Saddam Hussein. He *was* a bad man with a poor human rights
record. He *did* order his army to occupy Kuwait illegally, and
his actions *did* warrant international sanctions. But this reason-
ably accurate portrayal of Saddam Hussein wasn't sinister
enough to meet U.S. objectives. The U.S. National Security
State Establishment desperately wanted a war in order to fore-

close on the possibility of an authentically new world order based on nonviolent means of conflict resolution. The decision to seek a military confrontation in the Gulf was apparently made by President Bush within four days of Iraq's invasion of Kuwait.[8] By demonizing Saddam Hussein, the U.S. National Security Establishment not only reversed the political momentum calling for a "peace dividend," it also sought and to a great extent received "moral legitimacy" for the use of massive military force. The militarization of the Gulf crisis in turn helped to lay the foundation for the new world order the United States envisioned.

U.S. military leaders and the U.S. press treated attempts at a negotiated settlement as dangerous diversions that threatened a military outcome. The *Wall Street Journal* warned of "peace fever" after Saddam Hussein announced the freeing of all hostages in December 1990. "Saddam Hussein's bold, cynical but shrewd offer yesterday to release all hostages in Iraq," the paper noted without feigning objectivity, "suddenly increases the pressure for a negotiated settlement to the Middle East stand off. *That is the very outcome President Bush hoped to avoid.* . . . The hostage announcement has actually hardened the administration's resolve to keep . . . [military] pressure up." [Emphasis added.][9]

The press took a similar tact after the Soviet Union attempted to avert a ground war through diplomacy. Two *Los Angeles Times* reporters warned that events surrounding the Soviet peace initiative "imperil Bush's strategy" and threaten to "turn the Persian Gulf War into a game of diplomatic maneuvers. That could derail Bush's military plans to cut Saddam down to size, especially if it leads to lengthy and ambiguous negotiations."[10]

*Newsweek* took up a similar theme in March, in an article on the Gulf War entitled, "A Wrinkle in the New World Order: Soviet Moves in the Gulf Crisis Spell Trouble for Bush's Postwar Vision." The article says in part:

> In just a few frustrating days last week, the Soviet Union showed why Bush's dream of a new world order isn't likely to come true anytime soon. The problem with this latest incarnation of collective security . . . glides over the ques-

tion of who identifies the bullies—and who decides how to deal with them. Preaching "multilateralism" suggests to your partners that they have equal say in making those judgements and leaves you open to inconveniences like the Soviet peace proposals. . . . The reason the Soviet moves caught the White House off guard is that Bush has in mind a different concept: a world in which the United States leads, and the allies follow. It isn't a "new" order at all, but the same system the president and other men of his generation recall so nostalgically from the postwar period. It's the multilateralism of NATO, the IMF and the World Bank, where the United States paid the bills and called the shots. It's the model of the Korean War, which took place under U.N. auspices and included 16 nations but was always an American production. After all the months spent hammering out U.N. resolutions before the war began, Bush showed what his new order boils down to in responding to the Soviet plan: he decided on a get-out-by-Saturday ultimatum, then quickly called the allies to get them on board.[11]

Before diplomacy was abandoned in favor of a military solution, Ambassador Abdallah al-Ashtal, Yemen's representative to the United Nations, was interviewed by James Paul in the *Middle East Report*. Abdallah al-Ashtal, who at the time chaired the U.N. Security Council, stressed that the *means* through which the Gulf crisis was resolved would enhance or undermine the possibility of a strengthened United Nations and an authentically new world order.

> *Paul*: Do you see the UN coming out of this crisis in a stronger position?
> *Abdallah al-Ashtal*: That will depend on the kind of solution. The clearest effort of the UN was the sanctions. The sanctions imposed on Iraq have no parallel in recent history—nothing comes in, nothing goes out. Iraq cannot go on forever without withdrawing. But of course it will take some time. If the withdrawal comes through the sanctions and their enforcement, and then a peace plan is imple-

mented, the UN—the world—will start a new era. If it is resolved by war, even if the US comes out on top, we will have the preponderance of one or more powers which will undermine the democratic structures of the United Nations. So the solution of this conflict by war will undermine the prospect of an international order that is peaceful and legal.

*Paul*: Perhaps the precedent set by a peaceful settlement could then be applied to other forms of occupation in the region and elsewhere.

*Abdallah al-Ashtal*: Exactly.[12]

The ambassador then stated the tragedy and purpose of U.S. policy: "This sweeping sanctions regime can force Iraq to withdraw. Recourse to war means that we are using the UN as a coverup to promote the interests of one country."[13]

The United States cynically manipulated the United Nations in pursuit of a new world order in which military solutions are preferred over diplomacy. On November 29 the United Nations Security Council passed Resolution 678 authorizing member states "to use all necessary means" to end Iraq's occupation of Kuwait. This resolution, according to Ambassador Abdallah al-Ashtal, was "one of the most dangerous resolutions that the UN Security Council has adopted in its history."[14] Resolution 678 refused to authorize the "use of force" against Iraq as the Bush administration had proposed. However, its substitute language of using "all necessary means" to end Iraq's occupation of Kuwait was vague and open to manipulation. The United States used it, according to Abdallah al-Ashtal, as a "blanket authorization" for U.S.-led military action.[15]

The United States justified its actions against Iraq by appealing to international law while at the same time it violated the Charter of the United Nations. Article 42 of the U.N. Charter permits sending U.N. forces into combat only under command of the United Nations Military Commission. This wasn't done. Also, although the United States repeatedly cited U.N. resolutions to justify military action against Iraq, these resolutions were often passed through coercion and bribery. James Webb, Navy Secretary during the Reagan administration, stated January 14, 1991, that he believed "we have been maneuvered into war by the Bush administration." He dismissed U.S. efforts to justify its actions in light of U.N. resolutions. "We bought and paid for those resolutions," he said. Secretary of State James Baker "used our money, taxpayers' money, to do it."[16]

Resolution 678, according to Congressman Henry Gonzalez, Chairman of the House Banking Committee, was possible because President Bush unlawfully "bribed, intimidated, and threatened" U.N. Security Council members to force their support. U.S. actions, according to Gonzalez, included:

- forgiving a multibillion dollar debt of Egypt;
- approving a $140 million loan to China;
- promising $7 billion in economic aid to the Soviet Union;
- promising military assistance to Colombia;
- promising debt relief and military aid to Zaire;
- promising $12 billion in arms sales to Saudi Arabia;
- threatening Yemen with aid cuts; and,
- paying off $187 million of U.S. debt owed to the United Nations.[17]

One U.S. leader informed Yemen officials that the Security Council Resolution vote would be "the most expensive vote you'll ever take."[18] The day after it cast a no vote, Yemen received word of the termination of all U.S. aid. "There were all kinds of pressures," Yemen's ambassador to the United Nations stated. "It was inconceivable that some members of the Security Council would vote for a resolution to use force which was not based on an article of the U.N. Charter, and by troops which were not under the command of the Security Council."[19]

U.S. actions to coerce the United Nations and to militarize the Gulf crisis provide further evidence that we are facing a constitutional crisis within a National Security State. On January 16, 1991, Congressman Gonzalez introduced legislation to impeach President Bush for actions violating the U.S. Constitution:

From August 1990, through January 1991 the President embarked on a course of action that systematically eliminated every option for peaceful resolution of the Persian Gulf crisis. Once the President approached Congress for a declaration of war, 500,000 American soldiers' lives were in jeopardy—rendering any substantive debate by Congress meaningless. ... In contravention of the written word, the spirit, and the intent of the U.S. Constitution [President Bush] has declared that he will go to war regardless of the views of Congress and the American people.[20]

U.S. Middle East envoy Richard Armitage made it clear that the Constitution was an impediment to U.S. interests. Congress should not impede the president's exercise of power in a new world order in which the United States is perhaps the only world power:

Our Founding Fathers, reflecting their profound distrust of the tendency of governments to abuse their powers, devised a system in which those powers were divided and deliberately set at cross purposes. These "checks and balances" were created at a time when the United States was anything but a world power. Now that we are a world power—perhaps the only one—there is ample opportunity in our executive branch to bemoan "congressional meddling" in foreign policy. ... Congress should give our one nationally elected leader maximum leeway in crafting an honorable outcome.[21]

### Winners and Losers

There were many casualties of the Gulf War. More than a hundred thousand Iraqis died in the fighting; millions of Kurds, whom the United States encouraged to rise up against Saddam Hussein, became refugees; burning oil wells, oil spills, and damage to the fragile desert ecology threatened environmental catastrophe; once restored to his throne, the Emir of Kuwait began cracking down on opposition groups demanding democratic reforms; human rights officials noted that Kuwaiti military and resistance forces were routinely raping women and torturing and slaying suspected collaborators; and the post-war U.S. regional "peace initiative" seemed to be floundering.

In March 1991 the U.N. Security Council lifted its embargo on food supplies and some other humanitarian goods to Iraq noting that allied bombing had inflicted "near-apocalyptic" damage to Iraq's economy and threatened its people with "imminent catastrophe." Later that month officials from UNICEF reported that as a result of the Gulf War five million children in the Middle East and Gulf area risk spending their crucial formative years in deprived circumstances. Richard Reid, UNICEF director for North Africa and the Middle East, warned of a lost generation of children who are not direct victims of the conflict, but of its economic devastation.[22] In May a Harvard medical team estimated that at least 170,000 more Iraqi children would die throughout the year as a result of typhoid, cholera, malnutrition, and other health problems caused by the Gulf War than would have died under normal conditions.[23]

Dr. H. Jack Geiger, with Boston-based Physicians for Human Rights, returned from Iraq in April warning of a "slow motion catastrophe" overtaking the country. "We refer to this as a bomb now, die later kind of war," he said. "The four horsemen of the apocalypse — war, famine, disease and death — are riding through Iraq now."[24] The plight of two million Kurds was the most pressing issue, Geiger said, with from four hundred to one thousand dying each day. Most of the dead were children succumbing to dehydration brought on by diarrhea. However, while the world paid close attention to the plight of the Kurds it was ignoring a potentially far greater tragedy in Iraq. "Iraq," Dr. Jonathan Fine of Physicians for Human Rights warned, "is on the verge of starvation."[25]

This litany of human tragedy is the legacy of the Gulf War. However, it tarnished the war's luster only a little. Lance Morrow, in a post-war reflection in *Time*, noted that "Americans almost unconsciously regard the victory as a kind of moral cleansing: the right thing. But reality and horror have not been rescinded." Earlier in the essay he wrote:

> It is not inconsequential to kill 100,000 people. That much life suddenly and violently extinguished must leave a ragged hole somewhere in the universe. . . . The victors have not given them much thought. Still killing 100,000 people

is a serious thing to do. It is not equivalent to shooting a rabid dog, which is, down deep, what Americans feel the war was all about, exterminating a beast with rabies. . . . They were ordinary people: peasants, truck drivers, students and so on. They had the love of their families, the dignity of their lives and work. . . . The secret of much murder is to dehumanize the victim, to make him alien, to make him Other, a different species. . . . To kill 100,000 people and to feel no pain at having done so may be dangerous to those who did the killing. It hints at an impaired humanity.[26]

The problems so evident in the post–Gulf War period, even when acknowledged, leave two basic truths unspoken. These truths can be captured in one sentence: *The U.S. military committed some of modern history's most serious war crimes in a war that was fought because of the imperatives of a National Security State.*

The issue of U.S. war crimes will remain hidden. It is a charge reserved for losers, not victors. However, there are at least two areas in which the charge of war crimes applies to U.S. conduct in the war. First, the targets of U.S. bombing in Iraq included power plants, water plants, fuel supplies, and communications systems. By arguing that these were military targets, the United States ignored their vital importance to the survival of civilians who are supposed to be protected under the Geneva Conventions. The "slow motion catastrophe" overtaking Iraq, of which the Physicians for Human Rights warned, was the result of U.S. precision bombing, which destroyed the basic infrastructure on which life depends. For example, without power

You can't pump water, you can't purify water, you can't pump sewage, you can't irrigate the crops . . . you can't even count the sick and dying. . . . You have to imagine Chicago with people drinking sewage out of the Chicago River and trying to boil it with little kerosene stoves that can blow up. . . . They are caught in a high-technology trap. The infrastructure on which they depended for their lives has been explicitly and selectively destroyed.[27]

The other war-crimes issue has to do with excessive, brutal murder that goes beyond "normal" killing in war. Warfare, itself repulsive, provides opportunity for repulsive behavior and brutality. One marine returning to the United States told his local paper that "at camp, in the field, we'd shoot blanks. When we actually started shooting live rounds, and watching people drop," he continued, "it was like hunting the ultimate game in life. I had a good time," he said. "I really did. It sounds sadistic but it was the greatest feeling. Everybody'd been waiting, and once it started, we didn't want it to stop."[28] He was not the only one who didn't want the war to end. The allied commander, General H. Norman Schwarzkopf, lamented President Bush's decision to end the war, saying the United States had passed up the opportunity to make the war "a battle of annihilation."[29]

While war crimes cannot be based on the sadistic attitudes of soldiers and generals, they can be based on evidence of conduct in prosecuting the war. The specific issue of war crimes in this context has to do with U.S. bombing of retreating Iraqi soldiers as they evacuated Kuwait. *Newsday* reporters who raised the issue of excessive force wrote of retreating Iraqi troops:

> They were bombed repeatedly by U.S. planes and attacked by U.S. troops while doing what the United States had originally demanded—getting out of Kuwait. . . . Iraqi vehicles, some flying white flags, were backed up for miles on roads heading home when they were attacked over and over again by airplanes dropping antipersonnel bombs, then finished off by B-52 bombing runs. "Like shooting fish in a barrel" one pilot operating from the aircraft carrier Ranger described his morning's work.[30]

The other unspoken truth is that the numerous tragedies of the Gulf War and its aftermath, including U.S. war crimes, were products of a war that should never have been fought. General Schwarzkopf returned to a hero's welcome to address a joint session of Congress on May 8, 1991. "We were the thunder and lightning of Desert Storm," he shouted. "We were the United States military and damn proud of it." He then repeated the greatest deception of the Gulf War:

We left our homes and our families and traveled thousands of miles away and fought in places whose names we could not pronounce simply because you asked us to, and it therefore became our duty, because that's what your military does.

The war in the Gulf was the product of a National Security State. The U.S. military and National Security Establishment did not respond to a Congressional call. It created and manipulated a crisis. It wasn't a war fought to free Kuwait, to uphold international law, to demonstrate that big countries can't bully little ones, to usher in a new world order of peace and stability. It was fought by and for the U.S. military and the broader National Security Establishment.

A brief examination of whose interests were served by the Gulf War demonstrates that the military and broader National Security Establishment were the biggest winners. In my view there were six principle reasons for the Gulf War.

*One reason, although not the most important, is oil.* Two-thirds of the world's known oil reserves are located in the Middle East. The U.S. State Department has called this oil "a stupendous source of strategic power" and "one of the greatest material prizes in world history."[31] The United States is committed to maintaining control over governments in the region who exercise nominal control over the resources within their borders. Saddam Hussein, despite a long history of human rights abuses, was a favored U.S. ally until he demonstrated that he could not be trusted to follow U.S. directives. Middle Eastern oil is important to the United States in another way as well. Japan and Western Europe are far more dependent on oil from this region than the United States. As the United States sinks further behind these economic powerhouses it hopes to use its control over Middle Eastern oil supplies as leverage against its allies.

*A second factor contributing to the Gulf War is U.S. dependency on surplus oil revenues from the Middle East.* The Gulf War occurred in the context of huge U.S. budget deficits, the Savings and Loan scandal, a deeper crisis affecting the U.S. banking industry, and the beginning of an economic recession. Middle

East expert Joel Beinin describes the importance of recycled petro-dollars to the U.S. economy:

> Both the Saudis and the Kuwaitis pursue a policy of recycling petro-dollars in the economies of Western Europe and North America. That means that most of the profits that are made from the sale of oil by the Kuwaitis and by the Saudis are reinvested in the stock market, in the purchase of real estate, in the purchase of United States government treasury bonds. . . . Saudi Arabia has about $400 billion invested in the economies of Western Europe and North America and Kuwait has between $100 and $150 billion invested in those economies. Since the mid-1980s . . . Kuwait's income from its investment portfolio has been larger than its income from the sale of oil.[32]

The United States is committed to maintaining governments in the Middle East and elsewhere that are committed to highly unequal societies. Saddam Hussein, like all the other leaders in the region, ruled in a dictatorial fashion. This was not a problem for the United States. Iraq squandered enormous wealth in the war with Iran. This also was not a problem, because Iran was an enemy of the West and because the war lined the pockets of arms manufacturers. Iraq was a problem because its oil revenues belonged to the state and not to royal families. It provided universal health and education programs for its people, and Saddam Hussein was inflaming Arab masses by raising uncomfortable issues concerning inequalities within and between various countries in the region. For example, Saudi Arabia, according to a report from the United Nations Development Program, is thirty-second in per capita income but ranks sixty-ninth in the United Nation's human development index because of its poor educational system and pronounced inequalities in wealth distribution. Sri Lanka, the report notes by way of contrast, has per capita income fifteen times less than that of Saudi Arabia but has a higher adult literacy rate.[33] In short, the United States defends governments that maintain highly unequal societies because they use "surplus" oil revenues to finance the U.S. budget deficit and U.S. businesses and banks rather than to improve the living standards of the majority of their impoverished populations.

*The third reason for the Gulf crisis was that it took attention away from domestic problems.* Washington Post columnist David Broder offered the following explanation as to why so little attention was paid to a deepening recession:

> Why has it taken so long for something so obvious on Main Street to be recognized on Pennsylvania Avenue? You can blame much of the inattention on the Persian Gulf crisis. Kuwait and Saddam Hussein became the preoccupation of the president and his top advisors, the Congress and the mass media, consuming time and energy that would otherwise have been spent on the slump. The boom on Wall Street also masked the urgency that might otherwise have been felt about the drop in retail sales and manufacturing.[34]

Broder almost got it right when he suggested a relationship between the Gulf War and the recession. However, he ignored one important detail: The recession began one month *before* the beginning of the Gulf crisis. The Gulf War fulfilled part of its intended purpose when it diverted attention, not only from the recession, but from a far deeper economic crisis in which "the boom on Wall Street" had little relationship to the actual economic health of the country.

*A fourth reason for the Gulf War was intimidation.* General Colin Powell, on the eve of the U.S. invasion of Panama, reportedly said that "we have to put a shingle outside our door saying superpower lives here no matter what the Soviets do, even if they evacuate from all of Eastern Europe."[35] The Gulf War, like Panama, sent a clear message to friends and foes alike. "The U.S. war in the Persian Gulf," writes James Petras, "was an attempt to recreate Washington's role as world policeman, to re-subordinate Europe to U.S. power and to intimidate the Third World into submission."[36] The war not only intimidated third-world leaders who thought they might have more freedom to maneuver in the aftermath of the Cold War; it also sent a clear message to Europe: economic power may be important but it is military power that guarantees global predominance.

Michael Klare writes that "what made the Gulf War so distinctive, was the widespread (and often experimental) use of a new breed of munitions designed to duplicate the destructive effects of tactical nuclear weapons." These munitions, including fuel air explosives, penetration bombs, and widespread area cluster bombs, "were dropped in great profusion to destroy fortifications, demolish underground bunkers, disable tanks and vehicles, and kill or maim military personnel."[37] The effective demonstration of the destructive power and in some cases the precision of these weapons sent a clear message that no world order could be conceived of or hoped for that wasn't controlled and dominated by the United States.

*The fifth reason for the Gulf crisis was to foreclose on the peace dividend.* Andrew and Leslie Cockburn write:

> Short-term domestic political considerations aside, there were very important institutional imperatives behind the push toward military confrontation in the Gulf. . . . In April 1990 a seasoned Pentagon official lamented in casual conversation that the atmosphere at his place of employment was dire. "No one knows what to do over here," he sighed. "The [Soviet] threat has melted down on us, and what else do we have? The Navy's been going up to the Hill to talk about the threat of the Indian Navy in the Indian Ocean. Some people are talking about the threat of the Colombian drug cartels. But we can't keep a $300 billion budget afloat on that stuff. There's only one place that will do as a threat: Iraq." Iraq, he explained, was a long way away, which justified the budget for military airlift. It had a large air force, which would keep the United States Air Force happy, and the huge numbers of tanks in Saddam's army were more than enough to satisfy the requirements of the U.S. ground forces.[38]

This indicates that Iraq was targeted by the U.S. National Security Establishment as a useful enemy months before Iraq's invasion of Kuwait. The Gulf crisis as it unfolded proved so successful in eliminating the peace dividend that within the Pentagon "Desert Shield" was referred to as "Budget Shield."[39]

The goal of undermining the peace dividend was actually achieved without firing a shot. The budget agreements reached between Congress and the White House in the fall of 1990, just months into the crisis and long before any actual fighting, stipulated that not one penny of the military budget could be transferred to other programs for a period of at least three years. This "budget compromise" seemed to make war less likely because the National Security Establishment had already undone the peace dividend that only months before appeared certain. However, this perspective didn't account for just how badly the military wanted and needed a war, and how much President Bush was determined to seize the Gulf crisis and shape a world order based on U.S. military power.

Otis Pike, who spent fourteen years on the House Armed Services Committee, describes interservice rivalry as one of the dynamics of a war led by a National Security State. Pike argued in a pre-ground war article that the ground war, like the war itself, was the product of institutional imperatives. Each branch of the military services had to demonstrate its importance to post–Cold War conflicts:

> President Bush has said repeatedly that if America is "forced" to launch a land campaign in the Persian Gulf the decision will be a military one, not a political one. This is the right thing to say ... but it dismisses too casually one of the most pervasive political issues that never goes away. The issue is military politics. Not our military against their military, but our military against our military. ... There is a great deal of infighting ... among the various services for prestige, power and, most of all, money. If the Army gets too much money, the Navy and the Air Force get less. The more money the Marines get, the less the Army seems to need. ... Which brings us to the Persian Gulf. When we were enforcing the U.N. resolutions with a naval blockade only, the Navy did a grand job. We will never know whether it would have worked if given time. We do know that if it had, the Navy would have gotten all the credit. When the president decided to launch the air

war, the Air Force did a magnificent job. Whether air power and naval power alone are enough to do the job if given time we may never know. We do know that if they did, the Air Force and the Navy would get all the credit and all the prestige. If air power and sea power alone can win wars, what would happen to the Army's budget? Gen. Powell remains an Army man. He already has testified that air power and naval power alone can't do the job. We cannot escape politics in decisions about war, even military decisions.[40]

*This leads to the final reason for the Gulf War: the desire of the National Security Establishment to create a world order in which U.S. military power guarantees superpower status.* The Gulf War reestablished the primacy of the military in U.S. and global affairs. Senator John McCain of Arizona, eight months prior to the Iraqi invasion of Kuwait, argued that the United States had an enforcer role to play in the post–Cold War period. "No other allied nation will suddenly develop power projection forces, and . . . it would not be in our interest to encourage other nations to assume this role," he wrote in the *Armed Forces Journal*. "The U.S. may not be the 'world's policeman,' but its power projection forces will remain the free world's insurance policy."[41]

The Gulf War solidified this role for the United States in the new world order. The London *Financial Times* stated as events unfolded in November that the Gulf crisis was a "watershed event in U.S. international relations" that would turn "the U.S. military into an internationally financed public good." In the 1990s there was no alternative to "the U.S. military assuming a more explicitly mercenary role than it has played in the past."[42]

The financial editor for the *Chicago Tribune* argued at about the same time that the United States should exploit its "virtual monopoly on the security market . . . as a lever to gain funds and economic concessions" from Germany and Japan. The United States had "cornered the West's security market" and could act as "the world's rent-a-cops." He noted that some would call us "Hessians," a reference to German mercenaries fighting with British soldiers during the American revolution, but "that's a terribly demeaning phrase for a proud, well-trained, well-financed and well-respected military." The United States might have trouble economically competing with our less militaristic allies but "we should be able to pound our fists on a few desks" in Japan and Europe, and "extract a fair price for our considerable services." The United States could demand that they "buy our bonds at cheap rates, or keep the dollar propped up, or better yet, pay cash directly into our Treasury." A different role for the United States might be possible "but with it would go much of our control over the world economic system."[43]

Thomas Friedman, writing in *The New York Times* in June 1991, also highlighted the economic utility of U.S. military power. He indicated that establishing U.S. military predominance in a restructured NATO alliance was important because "the alliance is both a tool of American power politics and a stabilizer of politics within Europe." He noted that President Bush would have to work hard to convince U.S. families and taxpayers that U.S. soldiers were still needed in Europe despite an end of the Cold War. "For Americans, NATO's strongest selling point is that it provides a vehicle through which Washington exerts its military weight in Europe," he wrote, " . . . and this, as one American diplomat at NATO said, allows the Americans to 'tell the Europeans what we want on a whole lot of issues—trade, agriculture, the Gulf, you name it.' "[44]

Michael Klare describes what it means for the United States to maintain its "superpower status" in light of its decision to forego economic revitalization and assume the role of global enforcer:

[To be a superpower] according to the national security leadership of the United States is to assume leadership in the struggle against the South [and] to assume responsibility for the protection of the Western World's economic resources in return for the continuing profession of our leadership by our esteemed erstwhile allies in Europe and Japan who will continue to need us because we will protect their supply of oil and other strategic raw materials.[45]

Just how entrenched the role of global cop had become after the U.S. "victory" in the Gulf was illustrated in a single sentence in *Newsweek*: "The idea that economic power is what counts most in today's world, so fashionable before this war began, now seems woefully shortsighted."[46]

## Conclusion

During and after the war against Iraq, the United States grounded its actions in rhetoric of high moral purpose. Peace, justice, international cooperation, and diplomacy were to be the fruits of this war and the new world order in process of formation. However, the means employed point elsewhere. If the war against Iraq serves as a guide, then the new world order the United States is constructing prefers military solutions, scorns diplomacy, selectively obeys and enforces international law, respects human rights only when politically expedient, vilifies enemies, censors the press (which seems all too willing to confine its role to that of patriotic cheerleader), promotes uncritical patriotism, cultivates religious legitimacy, and manipulates the United Nations. It is also thoroughly racist and is willing to inflict unprecedented violence on third-world countries of "strategic" importance to the United States and other industrial nations of the North.

The U.S. National Security Establishment was the only clear winner in the Gulf War. With stunning speed it erased the prospects for a significant peace dividend; fashioned a world order based on "military power projection" rather than negotiations; carried out a press-sanctioned and presidentially-led "military coup"; intimidated potential adversaries and discouraged alternative visions of an authentically new order; showcased weapons and thereby dramatically improved prospects for global weapons sales; garnered support for other weapons systems, such as "star wars"; paved the way for a permanent U.S. military presence in the Gulf; and made significant strides in overcoming the Vietnam Syndrome.

The victory was both illusionary and costly. The cracks in the U.S. economy grew wider during the Gulf War and hopes for economic revitalization and the creation of an authentically new world order vanished. The U.S. and third-world poor were relegated to places of permanent marginalization. The United

States set a course for itself rooted in violence. U.S. democracy also failed a crucial test; it was now clearly subordinate to the priorities of a National Security State.

It would be difficult to imagine a more tragic or ironic scene than General Schwarzkopf, a representative of the National Security Establishment that had successfully carried out what amounted to a military coup, receiving standing ovations from Congressional members in the House Chamber. It was a scene reminiscent of Mark Twain's *War Prayer*, quoted at the beginning of the chapter. According to one reporter:

> The mood in the House chamber was upbeat and celebratory, with the Army Band playing patriotic tunes and military songs while the general made his way through backslapping, hand-shaking admirers representing both parties and various points on the political spectrum.[47]

There was one more casualty of the Gulf War—and even the National Security Establishment cannot long avoid the fallout from its wounds. The earth itself was crying out for healing, and the Gulf War placed serious obstacles in the path to survival.

CHAPTER 7

# Environmental Disorder

## in the Brave New World Order

*The more stitches the less riches. . . . Ending is better than mending.*

— Aldous Huxley, *Brave New World*

*The trends of environmental degradation . . . all continue unabated: Forests are shrinking, deserts expanding, and soils eroding. The depletion of the stratospheric ozone layer that protects us from harmful ultraviolet radiation appears to have escalated. The levels of carbon dioxide and other heat-trapping gases in the atmosphere continue to build in an all too predictable fashion. Only a monumental effort can reverse the deterioration of the planet.*

— Worldwatch Institute, *State of the World 1990*

The end of the Cold War is one of the most important events in human history. Its unexpected end came as the U.S. economy was collapsing under the weight of military priorities and individual and corporate greed; as living standards were deteriorating for poor people in the United States and throughout the Third World; and as the earth itself was threatened by environmental degradation. "Only a monumental effort can reverse the deterioration of the planet." This sobering ecological assessment

94

is a lens through which to judge the new world order being shaped in the post–Cold War period.[1]

The peace dividend was not only important to the revitalization of the U.S. economy; it also had profound implications for the survival of the planet. "As the East-West ideological conflict wanes," the Worldwatch Institute's report *State of the World 1990* noted hopefully, "it will free the time and energy of political leaders to concentrate on environmental threats to security. It will also facilitate a reordering of priorities, providing resources to reforest the earth, stop population growth, and develop energy resources that will stabilize the earth's climate."[2]

If the end of the Cold War is one of the most important events in world history, then the Gulf War is one of history's greatest disasters. The end of the Cold War could have inaugurated, as the Worldwatch Institute report stated, "a monumental effort" to overcome poverty and to "reverse the deterioration of the planet." However, the U.S. National Security Establishment used the Gulf War to steal the peace dividend, to forsake the path of economic renewal, and to establish a new world order characterized by U.S. military power, economic exploitation, and environmental degradation. The triumph of the U.S. National Security Establishment ultimately may be at the expense of the earth and all its inhabitants.

## Signs of Environmental Crisis

Herman E. Daly and John B. Cobb, Jr., describe the underlying similarities and environmental shortcomings of both capitalism and socialism:

> The conflict between capitalism and socialism is not about the desirability or possibility of industrialism. That is taken for granted by both sides. The conflict is over which economic system can better produce a growing quantity of goods and services and equitably spread the benefits of the industrial mode of production. Whatever their ideological differences both systems are fully committed to large-scale, factory-style energy and capital-intensive, specialized production units that are hierarchically managed. They also

rely heavily on nonrenewable resources and tend to exploit renewable resources and waste absorption capacities at nonsustainable rates.[3]

There are no countries or blocs, from the standpoint of environmental integrity, that can claim victory in the Cold War. The bureaucratically driven command economies of the Soviet Union and Eastern Europe left a legacy of environmental degradation. Energy inefficiency, reliance on coal, and few pollution controls led to deteriorated air and water quality, poor human health, and declining agricultural production. The free-market capitalist societies, which equate meaning with consumption and economic health with gross national product (GNP), exact equally serious environmental costs. In many third-world countries the integrity of the environment is one more casualty of IMF debt-regulated economies and the skewed development paths pursued by third-world elites.

*State of the World 1990* and *State of the World 1991*, produced by Worldwatch Institute, provide a sobering summary of a deep environmental crisis that demands an immediate and far reaching response. The signs of crisis include:

*Deforestation.* During the past twenty years the world has lost nearly 440 million acres of tree cover, an area the size of the United States east of the Mississippi River. The world's forests are shrinking at a rate of 37.4 million acres a year.

*Desertification.* Deserts expanded by 264 million acres from 1970 to 1990. This is an area larger than land devoted to food crops in China.

*The loss of topsoil.* Soil erosion is a major problem within the United States and many other countries. The earth has lost nearly one-fifth of its topsoil from its cropland. Each year approximately 13 million acres of land loses its productive potential and becomes wasteland.

*Extinction of plant and animal species.* Tens of thousands of the earth's plant and animal species have been destroyed over the past several decades due to human encroachment on fragile ecological systems.

*Air pollution.* During the 1980s the amount of carbon released into the earth's atmosphere from the burning of fossil fuels reached new highs, nearly six billion tons in 1990. Air pollution reduces U.S. crop production by five to ten percent and has a similar impact elsewhere. According to one estimate, polluted air costs the United States as much as $40 billion annually in health care and lost productivity. Air pollution in industrial countries throughout the world contributes to acid rain. For example, half of the seven hundred thousand lakes in the six eastern provinces of Canada are extremely acid sensitive.

*Climate change and global warming.* High fossil fuel related carbon emissions coupled with use of chlorofluorocarbons in products such as air conditioners and refrigerators are changing the earth's climate. Global warming, the result of the so-called greenhouse effect, threatens to undermine food production and to place wetlands, coastal forests, and cities at risk as sea levels gradually rise. If projections of future global warming and sea level rises are realized, present U.S. coastal wetlands will be reduced as much as eighty percent and coastal cities in many parts of the world will be under water.

*Reduced agricultural potential and productivity.* A growing scarcity of productive cropland, competition over use of limited fresh water, and environmental degradation pose serious obstacles to sustainable food production. A global downturn in per capita grain output is evident in every geographic area of the world. In both Latin America and Africa food consumption per person is lower today than it was a decade ago.

*Population growth.* World population is projected to grow by 960 million people in the decade of the 1990s. Population pressures in many poorer countries coupled with excessive consumerism among affluent groups in wealthy countries add to already serious environmental problems.

Environmental problems, largely ignored by economists, are beginning to have an impact on present and future economic productivity. "Throughout our lifetimes, economic trends have shaped environmental trends, often altering the earth's natural resources and systems in ways not obvious at the time," writes Lester Brown. "Now, as we enter the nineties, the reverse is also beginning to happen: environmental trends are beginning to shape economic trends." Reading the newspapers can be deceptive, according to Brown, because they give "the impression that changes in economic indicators such as the gross national product (GNP), interest rates, or stock prices are the keys to the future. But it is changes in the biological product that are shaping civilization."[4] Brown provides a summary of the environmental crisis and how it is often ignored by traditional economic planners:

> Anyone who regularly reads the financial papers or business weeklies would conclude that the world is in reasonably good shape and that long-term economic trends are promising. ... Yet on the environmental front, the situation could hardly be worse. Anyone who regularly reads scientific journals has to be concerned with the earth's changing physical condition. Every major indicator shows a deterioration in natural systems: forests are shrinking, deserts are expanding, croplands are losing topsoil, the stratospheric ozone layer continues to thin, greenhouse gases are accumulating, the number of plant and animal species is diminishing, air pollution has reached health-threatening levels in hundreds of cities, and damage from acid rain can be seen on every continent.[5]

## The Environmental Crisis and Third-World Poverty

The Gulf War and the new world order it reflects are disastrous when measured against the imperatives of ecological integrity and planetary survival. This is true for two reasons. First, reversing the deterioration of the planet depends on overcoming poverty. Second, economic renewal and environmental sustainability depend on wresting power from military sectors.

The new world order is being structured, instead, to continue a pattern of huge wealth transfers from the third-world poor to the first-world rich. "For the poor, particularly in Africa and Latin America," writes Alan Durning, "the eighties were an unmitigated disaster, a time of meager diets and rising death rates."[6] The so-called new order, which reinforces third-world poverty and global inequalities, aggravates an environmental crisis that ironically threatens both rich and poor alike. Lloyd Timberlake's dire assessment of Africa describes the future of many third-world peoples and perhaps the future of all peoples within the framework of the new world order. Africa, writes Timberlake, "has overdrawn its environmental accounts," leading to "environmental bankruptcy." "Bankrupt environments lead to bankrupt nations—and may ultimately lead to a bankrupt continent."[7]

Alan Durning describes the relationship between poverty and the destruction of the environment:

Destitution in the modern world is perpetuated by mutually reinforcing factors at the local, national, and international levels that form a global poverty trap. Poverty's profile ... has become increasingly environmental. The poor not only suffer disproportionately from environmental damage caused by those better off, they have become a major cause of ecological decline themselves as they have been pushed onto marginal land by population growth and inequitable development patterns. Economic deprivation and environmental degradation reinforce one another to form a maelstrom—a downward spiral that threatens to pull in ever more.[8]

Poor people are often forced by economic factors to degrade their environment. According to Durning:

Poverty drives ecological deterioration when desperate people overexploit their resource base, sacrificing the future to salvage the present. The cruel logic of short-term needs forces landless families to raze plots in the rain forest, plow steep slopes, and shorten fallow periods. Ecological decline, in turn, perpetuates poverty, as degraded ecosystems offer diminishing yields to their poor inhabitants. A self-feeding downward spiral of economic deprivation and ecological degradation takes hold.[9]

The problem of poor people degrading their environment is a direct product of the development path pursued by third-world elites and foreign economic interests. These groups encourage concentrated land holdings and marginalization of the poor, promote export agriculture at the expense of local food production, and favor urban-based elites at the expense of poor rural majorities and urban slum dwellers. Timberlake, citing British environmentalist Edward Goldsmith, notes that "governments, bilateral and multilateral aid agencies fail to see environmental stress as *symptomatic* of a social and political crisis, based on unequal access to land, conflict between export-based cash crops and basic food security, as well as short-term asset stripping for a quick profit."[10]

The economic realities that force poor people to degrade their environment similarly encourage the environmental pillaging of entire countries. For example, IMF structural adjustment programs (SAPs), with their emphasis on export-financed capital transfers from the Third World to first-world elites, are a major cause of environmental destruction throughout the Third World. "The massive diversion of resources to the North [through payments on the debt] has taken a toll not only on the people of developing lands, but on the land itself," Alan Durning writes. "Forests have been recklessly logged, mineral deposits carelessly mined, and fisheries overexploited, all to pay foreign creditors."[11] A year later the Worldwatch Institute's report notes:

> Lack of capital has made it nearly impossible for developing countries to invest adequately in forest protection, soil conservation, irrigation improvements, more energy-efficient technologies, or pollution control devices. Even worse, growing debts have compelled them to sell off natural resources, often their only source of foreign currency. Like a consumer forced to hock the family heirlooms to pay credit card bills, developing countries are plundering forests, decimating fisheries, and depleting water supplies — regardless of the long-term consequences.[12]

The new world order's IMF-imposed emphasis on export crops at the expense of peasant or campesino produced local foods forces the majority of third-world farmers onto marginal land. This is a prescription for malnutrition and environmental bankruptcy. Because reducing population growth depends on authentic development, it also contributes to rapid population growth, which within the cycle of poverty and unequal development becomes both a symptom and a cause of environmental decay.

Reducing population growth is an environmental imperative. Historical patterns demonstrate that the keys to overcoming poverty and reducing population growth are literacy, secure land rights, local control over economic resources, availability of credit, clean drinking water, effective primary health care, access to family planning, and strong grass-roots organizations.

In the state of Kerala, India, for example, an organized population has achieved major economic and social gains despite a per capita income that is only two-thirds of the average throughout India. A survey of a half-million Indian villages ranked Kerala first in fifteen of twenty categories measuring economic and social well-being. Economic reforms, including extensive land reform and the availability of basic goods at fair-price shops, have been linked to social priorities that benefit the poor. Kerala's citizens have easy access to health care, education, libraries, and clean water. Immunization and family-planning services are widely available. Kerala's adult literacy rate is nearly twice the national average, its people live approximately eleven years longer, its infant mortality rate is two-thirds lower, its birthrate is one-third lower, and inequalities between sexes and castes are less pronounced than in other states in India.[13]

These basic features of dignified life in a poor country among relatively poor people are living signs of hope. However, they are in conflict with the priorities of dominant world orders both past and present; the hallmarks of the IMF-policed new world order are deadly poverty, military power, and environmental decay. Alan Durning notes that "no impoverished nation can reform its economy sufficiently in the short term to compensate for massive debt burdens . . . and falling prices." These problems are aggravated by high interest rates in New York and unjust pricing policies in the international economy. "The economy that most needs adjustment," according to Durning, "is the global one."[14]

The architects of the new world order deny the interrelatedness of the human family and our common global environment. Yet overcoming global poverty is an important goal for all decent people. It is also an environmental imperative. Durning provides a compelling summary:

> No one can question that there is something morally bankrupt about a world where, amid extravagant abundance, one quarter of the human family is doomed to an unremitting battle for survival. But poverty is more than a moral issue. Failure to launch an all-out assault on poverty will not only stain the history of our age, it will guarantee the destruction of much of our shared biosphere. ... When the poor destroy ecosystems in desperation, they are not the only ones who suffer. ... The fate of the fortunate is immutably bonded to the fate of the dispossessed through the land, water and air: in an ecologically endangered world, poverty is a luxury we can no longer afford.[15]

## Environmental Destruction and the National Security State

Another reason for harshly judging the new world order is that the triumph of the U.S. National Security State, so evident in the Gulf War, undermines the possibility of economic renewal and environmental sustainability. Worldwatch Institute estimates that we have forty years to place the world on sound environmental footings.

> If the world is to achieve sustainability, it will need to do so within the next 40 years. If we have not succeeded by then, environmental deterioration and economic decline are likely to be feeding on each other, pulling us into a downward spiral of social disintegration.[16]

Worldwatch Institute points out that although third-world peoples contribute to global environmental problems, "most of the world's looming environmental threats, from groundwater contamination to climate change, are byproducts of affluence."[17] U.S. citizens, therefore, shoulder significant responsibility for the environmental crisis. Further, U.S. foreign policy imposes conditions on third-world peoples and nations that force them to degrade the environment. Our affluence, directly or indirectly, contributes to global poverty and to each major environmental problem. It is in this context of our special responsibility and our urgent need to change that the Gulf War looms as a potentially catastrophic event.

Reading Worldwatch Institute reports is an alternating journey between despair and hope. The reports portray a sobering picture of rapidly escalating environmental destruction and a well-articulated vision of a sustainable future. On the one hand, billions of human beings are condemned to death or poverty and an escalating environmental catastrophe is encircling the earth. On the other hand, a sustainable global economy, one that meets needs without sacrificing future generations, is both possible and desirable.

According to Worldwatch Institute, the sustainable global society of 2030 will have these characteristics:

• Solar energy will be the foundation of a sustainable world energy system. The world will have made a transition away from dependency on coal, oil, and natural gas and will reject nuclear power because of its economic, social, and environmental liabilities. Wind, hydropower, solar thermal power, solar panels, photovoltaic solar cells, geothermal plants, and energy crops grown on lands unsuitable for food production will be key components in a sustainable society based on renewable energy resources. "A typical urban landscape will have thousands of collectors sprouting from rooftops ... and passive solar architecture may by then cut artificial heating and cooling needs to virtually zero in millions of buildings."[18] The shift to a solar-based energy system will be of particular benefit to today's impoverished third-world peoples:

> The key advantage of photovoltaics is their versatility. They can be used not only in large electricity plants but to power small water pumps and rural communications systems. As they become economical, the completion of the solar revolution will be possible: all Third World villages can be electrified with this technology. Unlike communities today, these villages will not have to depend on extended

power lines connected to centralized plants. Rather they contain their own power sources.[19]

• There will be greater equality within and among nations. The burden of indebtedness will have eased as a matter of economic justice and environmental necessity. Third-world countries will have stabilized their populations and will have moved to ecologically sound development.

• The health and well-being of societies will not be judged by misleading indicators such as gross national product, stock prices, or growth in international trade. It will be measured in terms of human health, quality of life, equity, overcoming poverty, and environmental sustainability. "Contrary to what political leaders imply, global economic growth as currently pursued is not the solution to poverty," write Sandra Postel and Christopher Flavin. "Despite the fivefold rise in world economic output since 1950, 1.2 billion people—more than ever—live in absolute poverty. More growth of the sort engineered in recent decades will not save the poor; only a new set of priorities can."[20] In fact, the sustainable world of 2030 may actually move away from free trade and the massive production and movement of environmentally questionable products. It will stress decentralized development approaches that reflect environmental realities and take advantage of the wide dispersion of solar energy.

• Vast areas of land within both developed and developing countries will be reforested. Efforts to reduce wasteful use of wood products will be coupled with responsible forest management. Environmentally sound forestry will stress sustainable harvesting of lumber and species diversity, and will respect the role of forests in maintaining air and water quality.

• Energy will be used much more efficiently than in today's wasteful societies. Applying already available technologies could dramatically improve fuel use in autos, efficiency in lighting systems, and reduce the energy used to heat homes and power necessary industries. Using energy efficiently is important, but still more is required:

Improving energy efficiency will not noticeably change lifestyles or economic systems. A highly efficient refrigerator or light bulb provides the same service as an inefficient one—just more economically. Gains in energy efficiency alone, however, will not reduce fossil fuel carbon emissions by the needed amount. Additional steps to limit the use of fossil fuels are likely to reshape cities, transportation systems, and industrial patterns, fostering a society that is more efficient in all senses.[21]

• The principal source of materials for industry will be recycled goods, not virgin raw materials. Economies in the year 2030 will emphasize recycling, avoid nonessential materials in production and packaging, and limit production of goods which generate hazardous wastes.

• The availability of a diverse set of transportation options will dramatically reduce our dependence on automobiles. By 2030 only electric or hydrogen-powered vehicles will be permitted in cities, and they will be powered by solar power plants. City streets and paths will encourage bicycling and walking. Efficient light rail systems will allow people to move quickly between neighborhoods.

• Employment opportunities will reflect radically different economic and social priorities. People in 2030 will live close to where they work and in many cases "people may work at home or in special satellite offices, connected by electronic lines rather than crowded highways."[22] The shift away from fossil fuels to renewable energy sources, and from virgin resources to recycled ones, will mean fewer jobs in coal mining, auto production and service, mining, and oil. Job losses in these areas will be offset by employment gains in the manufacture and sale of wind turbines, bicycles, solar technologies, mass transit equipment, and numerous recycling technologies.

A far greater share of workers will be employed in repair, maintenance, and recycling activities than in the extraction of virgin materials and production of new goods. Wind prospectors, energy efficiency auditors, and solar architects will be among the booming professions. . . . Opportunities in forestry will expand markedly . . . as will specialists in biological methods of pest control. . . . Petroleum geologists may be retrained as geothermal geologists . . . while traditional midwives continue to broaden their roles to include the spectrum of family planning needs.[23]

• The transition to a sustainable society will be financed through taxes on products and activities that have a negative impact on the environment. This will force citizens to measure and pay for environmental costs reflected in private choices. Governments can move economies quickly in the direction of sustainability by raising a large proportion of revenue from such "green taxes."

• Materialism will not survive the transition to a sustainable world. Simpler, less consumptive lifestyles will be the norm in 2030. A society addicted to consumerism will find the transition to sustainability difficult. However,

> the potential benefits of unleashing the tremendous quantities of human energy now devoted to designing, producing, advertizing, buying, consuming, and discarding material goods are enormous. Much undoubtedly would be channeled into forming richer human relationships, stronger communities, and greater outlets for cultural diversity, music, and the arts.[24]

As materialism loses its grip, environmental values will replace a throwaway mentality among both consumers and producers. *Brave New World*'s ethic, "ending is better than mending," so symbolic of our own throwaway societies, will gradually disappear. Products will be judged worthy on the basis of utility, durability, and sustainability rather than convenience. Human worth will no longer be determined by excessive consumption; rather, alternative values and lifestyles will become the norm:

> The fundamental changes . . . in energy, forestry, agriculture, and other physical systems cannot occur without corresponding shifts in the social, economic, and moral character of human societies. During the transition to sustainability, political leaders and citizens alike will be forced to reevaluate their goals and aspirations, to redefine their

measures of success, and to adjust work and leisure to a new set of principles that have at their core the welfare of future generations. Given the enormity of the tasks involved, many people may assume that moving in this direction will be painful and limiting, and thus something to resist. But given the choice of repairing your house or having it collapse around you, you would not question whether to undertake the project.[25]

It would be difficult to overstate the dangers to planetary survival posed by the environmental fallout from present military, economic, and political priorities. The good news, according to Worldwatch Institute, is that although a monumental effort is required, a sustainable future is possible. The most sobering aspect of these reports is their repeated emphasis that the changes required to save the earth depend on the human and financial resources now wasted in military priorities. A sampling of quotations from Worldwatch Institute reports illustrates why I refer to the Gulf War, and the victory for the U.S. National Security State Establishment that it reflects, as one of the greatest disasters in human history:

As the nineties begin, the world is on the edge of a new age. The Cold War that dominated international affairs for four decades and led to an unprecedented militarization of the world economy is over. With its end comes an end to the world order it spawned. The East-West ideological conflict was so intense that it dictated the shape of the world order for more than a generation. ... But with old priorities and military alliances becoming irrelevant, we are now at one of those rare points in history—a time of great change. ... No one can say with certainty what the new order will look like. But if we are to fashion a promising future for the next generation, then the enormous effort required to reverse the environmental degradation of the planet will dominate world affairs for decades to come. In effect, the battle to save the planet will replace the battle over ideology as the organizing theme of the new world order.[26]

If the physical degradation of the planet becomes the principal preoccupation of the global community, then environmental sustainability will become the organizing principle of this new order. ... The world's agenda will be more ecological than ideological, dominated less by relationships among nations and more by the relationship between nations and nature.[27]

In the new age, diplomacy will be more concerned with environmental security than with military security. ... Political influence will derive more from environmental and economic leadership than from military strength. ... Leadership in the new order is likely to derive less from military power and more from success in building environmentally sustainable economies. The United States and the Soviet Union, the traditional military superpowers, are lagging badly in this effort and are thus likely to lose ground to those governments that can provide leadership in such a shift.[28]

Achieving an environmentally sustainable global economy is not possible without the fortunate limiting their consumption in order to leave room for the poor to increase theirs. With the ending of the Cold War and the fading of ideological barriers, an opportunity has opened to build a new world upon the foundations of peace. A sustainable economy represents nothing less than a higher social order—one as concerned with future generations as with our own, and more focused on the health of the planet and the poor than on material acquisitions and military might. While it is a fundamentally new endeavor, with many uncertainties, it is far less risky than continuing with business as usual. The basic elements involved in getting there are no mystery; all the needed technologies, tools, and instruments of change exist. The real hurdle is deciding to commit ourselves to a new path.[29]

Despite growing public concern, government expenditures to defend against military threats still dwarf those to protect us from environmental ones. For example, the United States plans to spend $303 billion in 1990 to protect the country from military threats but only $14 billion to protect from environmental threats, a ratio of 22 to 1.[30]

The Gulf War reestablished the predominant position of the U.S. National Security Establishment in U.S. and world affairs. In doing so it accelerated the global environmental crisis in numerous ways. *First, the Gulf War did serious damage to the fragile desert ecology of the region.* The "world's armed forces are quite likely the single largest polluter on earth," writes Michael Renner. "Modern warfare entails large-scale environmental devastation, as conflicts in Vietnam, Afghanistan, Central America and the Persian Gulf amply demonstrate."[31] The United States accused Iraq of "environmental terrorism" as oil well fires darkened the skies of Kuwait and oil leaked into the sea. It did so with little acknowledgment of its own role in the catastrophe. For example, *The New York Times* editorialized:

Saddam Hussein's decision to torch more than 600 oil wells in Kuwait, an act of insane vindictiveness, may yield his grimmest legacy. ... The fires are consuming five million barrels a day, three times Kuwait's prewar production. ... Oil covers thousands of acres, killing plant life and threatening subsurface water. Smoke turns day to night. ... The greatest threat is a temperature inversion that would keep the fumes at ground level, forcing many people to breathe toxic gases. ... The mist of oil also threatens to contaminate the Persian Gulf and the phytoplankton that nourish the region's fish. Some scientists even speculate that the hot fires will interfere with regional weather patterns and disrupt or deflect the July-August monsoons on which the nations of the Indian Ocean depend for water and food. The carbon dioxide released by the fire may not rise high enough to worsen the feared warming of the earth's atmosphere.

The *Times* neglected to say that any reasonable assessment of blame for the ecological disaster unfolding in the aftermath of the Gulf War must include the fact that serious environmental problems were a predictable outcome of a war that should never have been fought. The environment was one of many casualties as the United States manipulated a crisis, avoided diplomacy, and defended the institutional privileges of the National Security Establishment through war. The best the *Times* could do was to say that "calculations of environmental risk belong in future military planning and public debate preceding any decision to go to war. In the meantime a more vigorous effort is needed to alleviate the human suffering caused by Saddam Hussein's wanton destruction."[32]

*Second, the war in the Gulf reinforced U.S. dependency on oil and ensured that fossil fuels would remain the primary energy source within the new world order.* Tragically, one of the principal obstacles to global survival, according to the Worldwatch Institute, is that the world will not run out of oil fast enough to save the planet! The world now "faces a new set of limits," *State of the World 1990* reports in its final chapter. "Long before fossil fuels are exhausted, rising global temperatures from their use could spell an end to civilization as we know it."[33] Ironically, to the degree that the Gulf War helps us maintain our way of life, including wasteful consumption of oil and other resources, it increases the likelihood of our demise and the destruction of the planet we inhabit.

*A third example of environmental fallout is the degree to which President Bush's popularity during and following the Gulf War will enable him to pursue other environmentally destructive agendas.* For example, during the Gulf War President Bush announced his energy plan for the nation. It called for continued dependence on foreign oil, promoted incentives for wildcat drilling within the United States and in offshore areas, opened up the Arctic National Wildlife Refuge for oil operations, encouraged nuclear power, and stressed greater reliance upon natural gas. His energy plan gave little or no attention to conservation, renewable energy, or "green taxes." President Bush also proposed adding the equivalent of two interstate highway systems to the 44,000 mile network now in place, what Jane Holtz Kay called "an oil man's leap into the auto abyss."[34]

The president also capitalized on his Gulf-induced popularity by winning Congressional approval for "fast track" negotiations on a free-trade agreement with Mexico. This too has serious environmental implications. I described the vital need for the United States to revitalize its economy in Chapter 2. The United States, I noted, could improve its competitive position by redirecting priorities away from nonproductive sectors dominated by military spending and speculative investors. However, within the framework of the new world order, sectors of U.S. business are seeking to restore their competitive position by reducing the living standards of U.S. workers and by taking advantage of low wages available in third-world countries. Another means of regaining a competitive edge in the "new" order is to transfer costs to the environment. A free-trade agreement with Mexico, for example, would enable U.S. companies to take further advantage of both cheap labor and weak environmental standards. *Time*, in a May 1991 article, notes:

> In many places you can smell the border before you can see it. Some days an acrid brown cloud hangs over the city of El Paso in the U.S. and nearby Ciudad Juarez in Mexico. . . . A fetid creek . . . carries raw sewage from shantytowns south of the border. . . . In Matamoros . . . children and dogs play along ditches that are coated with an iridescent slick of aromatic chemicals, many of which are known or suspected carcinogens. . . . Over the past 10 years nearly 2,000 foreign-owned factories—most of them the property of U.S. corporations—have sprung up along the Mexican side of the . . . border. Attracted by low wages and lax pollution laws, these assembly plants . . . have drawn thousands of Mexicans into already crowded border cities, overwhelming meager municipal services and turning much of the region into a cesspool.

The article goes on to describe the likely implications of a free-trade zone:

> The key to the border region's explosive growth is an experimental free-trade zone created in the 1960s for foreign-owned companies wishing to assemble products for

the U.S. market. Parts brought into the zone are exempt from Mexican duties, and finished products sent back to the U.S. are taxed only on the value added by cheap Mexican labor. . . . The opponents of the free-trade pact have embraced the concerns of environmental groups, who say that without strict safeguards, the measure would be an invitation for U.S. companies to export their most polluting factories to Mexico. That is just what's happening now in the border region, according to a report issued last week by the National Toxic Campaign Fund. . . . In spot samples taken near Mexican industrial parks, scientists found evidence that 75% of the sites were discharging toxic chemicals directly into public waterways. Measurements taken near one plant owned by General Motors showed concentrations of xylene, a toxic solvent, 6,300 times as high as the standard for U.S. drinking water. An employee told the N.T.C.F. that the company regularly pours untreated solvents right down the drain. GM disputes the findings.[35]

*Finally, the Gulf War and the National Security State-led "new" order that it ushers in have robbed the world of a post–Cold War opportunity to tackle issues of global survival.* The triumph of the U.S. National Security State ensures that the military will remain the country's largest energy user and environmental polluter. For example, each year the Pentagon uses enough energy to run the entire U.S. mass transit system for fourteen years. More important, the National Security Establishment will squander precious human and financial resources to reinforce a global economic order that enables—at least for a time—a minority of affluent consumers to eat away at the earth's life-support system while forcing poor nations and poor people within them to degrade their environments.

## Conclusion

Time is short and the challenges that confront us are enormously complicated by the Gulf War and the power of the U.S. National Security State. The decisions we make in the next several years and decades will determine the viability of the planet.

I was forty years old when the Gulf War began and when I read *State of the World 1990*'s forty-year timetable for a transition to sustainable societies. It was sobering to realize that the fate of the earth and the world's children would likely be decided by the time my children, who are ages three and one, reach my present age. It was equally sobering to ponder how people of faith — through silence, complicity, or active participation — could celebrate the Gulf War and a new world order in which billions of people were condemned to poverty, the earth's survival was called into question, and the National Security Establishment reigned supreme.

## CHAPTER 8

# Mark, Jesus, and the Kingdom:

# Confronting World Orders, Old and New

*No one sews a piece of unshrunk cloth on an old cloak;
otherwise, the patch pulls away from it, the new from the old,
and a worse tear is made. And no one puts new wine into old
wineskins; otherwise, the wine will burst the skins, and the
wine is lost, and so are the skins; but one puts new wine into
fresh wineskins.*

—Mark 2:21-22

People of faith and churches within the United States bear
significant responsibility for the present crises of poverty, militarism, and environmental decay. The triumphalism that greeted
the Gulf War, the predominant position of the National Security
State Establishment within U.S. society, and the so-called new
world order based on poverty, militarism, and environmental
bankruptcy are possible in part because as individuals and as
churches we have been assimilated into a dominating culture
that clashes sharply with authentic Christian values. "The dominant values of American life," writes Marcus Borg "—affluence,
achievement, appearance, power, competition, consumption,
individualism—are vastly different from anything recognizably
Christian. As individuals and as a culture . . . , our existence has
become massively idolatrous."[1]

The gospel of Mark offers a compelling foundation from which to critique world orders old and new. Mark's story of Jesus emphasizes four themes of particular interest to Christians who are committed to an authentically new world order: confrontation with empire; conflict with the religious order that sanctions or contributes to the oppression of the poor; formation of alternative community; and challenges to and replacement of fundamental myths that lend legitimacy to an unjust order. This chapter explores these themes as well as the obstacles to discipleship evident in Mark that are relevant to our discipleship journey. The final chapter will explore how the gospel, if taken seriously, can lead people of faith and our churches out of captivity to freedom.

### Competing Gospels: The Confrontation with Empire

Mark initiates his story of Jesus with eight seemingly noncontroversial words: "The beginning of the Gospel of Jesus Christ. . . . " Surprisingly, these words turn the world of Mark's contemporaries upside down, and they can also subvert our world if we let them speak to us with something of their original power. *Gospel* was not primarily a religious term during the time of Jesus and Mark (Mark wrote his Jesus story between 30 and 40 years after the death of Jesus); it was a military propaganda term for the Roman empire.[2] The gospel was Rome's announcement of the "good news" of military conquest, the "good news" of the subjugation of peoples, the "good news" of another victory over rebellious territories, the "good news" of "benevolent" colonial rule commemorated with celebrations and festivals. Thus the first verse of Mark's gospel sets up an irreconcilable conflict between faith and empire.

Ched Myers writes:

> Mark is taking dead aim at Caesar and his legitimating myths. From the very first line, Mark's literary strategy is revealed as subversive. Gospel is not an inappropriate title for this story, for Mark will indeed narrate a battle. But the "good news" of Mark does not herald yet another vic-

tory by Rome's armies; it is a declaration of war upon the political culture of the empire.[3]

Conflict with Rome is rarely addressed head-on in Mark's gospel because he is living and writing in "occupied territory."[4] However, incompatibility between the kingdom of God and imperial Rome is implicit throughout. The appropriation of the term *gospel*, as I've already noted, is itself subversive. Mark's words "the beginning of the gospel" lead us back to the creation story in Genesis. The world is being re-created. This is bad news for the empire and for others who benefit from the injustices of the present order. The new creation ushered in by Jesus and the Spirit promises to overthrow the powers, including those of Rome. The call to discipleship is an invitation to confront empire, and the cost of discipleship inevitably includes the wrath of empire as it defends imperial priorities and power.

The explosive nature of competing gospel claims is illustrated by the fact that John the Baptist is arrested fourteen verses into Mark's story. John preaches the need for repentance and paves the way for Jesus' ministry. He is later murdered by Herod, Rome's appointed ruler. The Jewish historian Josephus describes the political reasons for John's death:

> Herod had John put to death, though he was a good man and had exhorted the Jews to live righteous lives, to practice justice towards their fellows and piety toward God. . . . When others too joined the crowds about him, because they were aroused to the highest degree by his words, Herod became alarmed. Eloquence that has so great an effect on the people might lead to some form of sedition, for it looked as if they would be guided by John in everything that they did. Herod decided, therefore, that it would be much better to strike first and be rid of him before his work led to an uprising, than to wait for an upheaval, get involved in a difficult situation, and see his mistake.[5]

The contemporary relevancy of a radical gospel confronting unjust political power is striking. The description of Herod's rationale for murdering John the Baptist could easily describe deliberations made by the murderers of Archbishop Romero in El Salvador.

John is not the only one in trouble early in the gospel account. By the end of the first chapter "Jesus could no longer openly enter a town" (Mk 1:45). Just two chapters later a powerful, and seemingly unlikely, coalition has formed: the Herodians along with their religious accomplices are plotting to murder Jesus, their common enemy (Mk 3:6).

Mark's double trial of Jesus (14:53-15:15) further emphasizes that he is murdered because he poses a threat to both Roman and Jewish political and religious authorities. Jesus is tried first by the Sanhedrin (a religious supreme court) and then before Pilate (a Rome-appointed governor). He is sentenced to death by Pilate and is crucified, a method of execution reserved for political crimes.

A final and compelling example of the inherent conflict between competing gospels, that is, between the good news of Jesus Christ and the "good news" of imperial conquest and propaganda, is the healing of the Gerasene demoniac found in Mark 5:1-13. Jesus encounters a man with an unclean spirit. "No one could bind him" and "no one had the strength to subdue him."

> And he shouted at the top of his voice, "What have you to do with me, Jesus, Son of the Most High God? I adjure you by God, do not torment me." For he [Jesus] had said to him, "Come out of the man, you unclean spirit!" Then Jesus asked him, "What is your name?" He replied, "My name is Legion; for we are many." He begged him earnestly not to send him out of the country. Now there on the hillside a great herd of swine was feeding; and the unclean spirits begged him, "Send us into the swine; let us enter them." So he gave them permission [dismissed them]. And the unclean spirits came out and entered the swine; and the herd, numbering about two thousand, rushed [charged] down the steep bank into the sea, and were drowned in the sea (Mk 5:7-13).

"Legion ... had only one meaning in Mark's social world: a division of Roman soldiers," according to Myers.

Alerted to this clue, we discover that the rest of the story is filled with *military* imagery. The term used for "herd" ... inappropriate for pigs, who do not travel in herds—often was used to refer to a band of military recruits. ... The phrase "he dismissed them" ... connotes a military command, and the pigs' charge ... into the lake suggests troops rushing into battle. ... Enemy soldiers being swallowed by hostile waters of course brings to mind the narrative of Israel's liberation from Egypt.[6]

Although Jesus was a Spirit-filled person, with healing an important aspect of his ministry and exorcisms common to the ancient world, there can be no doubt about the intended symbolism: the gospel of Jesus Christ portends the defeat of Rome. This story is particularly provocative in a context in which Rome routinely executed anyone suspected of challenging Roman domination. The inevitable conflict between the gospel of Jesus Christ and the imperial gospel should be deeply disturbing to us because we read Mark's story of Jesus situated in a modern-day empire.

## The Conflict with Religious Authorities

The conflict between Jesus and prominent religious authorities and structures of the dominant order is a second and equally challenging theme in Mark's gospel story. The church is an important institution in our society. However, faith is largely a matter of personal choice; churches are voluntary organizations, and church and state are formally separated. It is somewhat difficult, therefore, for us to appreciate fully the power religious institutions and authorities exercised over the lives of people during the time of Jesus. They directly and indirectly oppressed the poor and for this reason came into sharp conflict with Jesus.

The Jewish Temple was the center of political, economic, and religious life in a society dominated by poverty and oppression. The Temple, according to the prevailing worldview, was God's dwelling place, the point of contact between deity and humanity. The Temple establishment mediated relationships both between the people and God, and the people and Rome. In doing so it played a decisive role in all aspects of life. Politically, an elite sector of Jewish leaders centered around the high priest openly collaborated with Rome; economically, the Temple-based order contributed to the exploitation of the poor; and religiously, the Temple leaders defined the symbolic order that gave legitimacy to the unjust social system.

Political accommodation was a consequence of subservience to Rome. The high priest was appointed by and accountable to Roman authorities. He retained his power through the good graces of the empire and was expected to maintain order in unruly Palestine. The high priest balanced desires for Jewish national independence with the realities of Roman power. He did so under enormous pressure from religious reformers, who longed for the reestablishment of an independent Israel free from Roman domination and ruled by a Davidic-type king. These aspirations found expression in constant social tensions and numerous revolts and acts of resistance against Roman authorities and their Jewish collaborators, which culminated in the Jewish-Roman war of 66-70 C.E. This war, which resulted in the destruction of Jerusalem and the Temple, is the context in which Mark's gospel story is written.

The economic oppression of the poor in first-century Palestine was linked to the practices of imperial Rome and to the Temple-based economy dominated by religious elites. Roman domination of Palestine was an affront to national sovereignty for all Jews, rich and poor alike. However, for the impoverished rural majority, it meant economic hardship as Rome imposed various taxes and rents that could add up to fifty percent of the harvest.[7] The Temple-based economy centered in Jerusalem aggravated the already precarious situation of the poor.

The Temple also dominated the economic life of the rural population through a system of tithing and redistribution. Jewish farmers were subject to double taxation, as both Rome and the Temple demanded a share of peasant harvests. While Rome used police power to deter tax resisters, the Temple used ideological persuasion through control of the symbolic order: those who didn't tithe were treated as outcasts. The impact of the Jerusalem-based Temple economy extended beyond rural areas and affected the whole society. This was particularly evident around feast days. Bill Wylie Kellermann writes:

> By Torah interpretation the "second tithe" was to be consumed in Jerusalem. Pilgrims from a distance would convert the tithe to money and spend it at festival time. Around that grew further commerce and an urban service industry. Moreover, the Temple was a massive stockyard and slaughterhouse; as many as eighteen thousand lambs might be sacrificed in the ceremonies. Think of the Temple workers involved, the money changers and sellers of animals . . . but also the carpenters and construction workers in the building trades engaged in the luxurious rehabilitation of the Temple and its precincts. Seen in this light, Passover as the central feast is the source of jobs, income, commerce. Vested interests abide at several levels of class and status.[8]

The Temple's role in exploiting the poor was more a consequence of a deeply entrenched religious worldview and social order than it was a product of political collusion between Rome and accommodating Jewish elites. Due to the Temple's influence the exploitation of the poor would have been severe even apart from Roman domination. The leaders of the Temple solidified their political and economic power through control of the symbolic order of the society, which determined who was pure or impure, holy or sinful, honored or despised. This symbolic order was defined in relation to what Marcus Borg refers to as "the politics of holiness." Religious leaders in Israel, with long memories of the exile and in the context of ongoing Roman domination, defined a system of rules, regulations, and cultural norms designed to maintain the integrity of Israel while avoiding another outpouring of God's judgment. As a result, Borg notes, "the Jewish social world and its conventional wisdom became increasingly structured around the polarities of holiness as separation: clean and unclean, purity and defilement, sacred and profane, Jew and Gentile, righteous and sinner."[9]

Religious reform movements, such as the Essenes and Pharisees, in competition with the aristocratic Sadducees, defined particular and competing standards of fidelity to these norms and statutes based on their interpretation of the Hebrew Scriptures or oral tradition. The result was an elitist system that perpetuated a cycle of poverty and impurity that victimized the poor while shoring up the power of elite sectors. The "more intense the demands of holiness became (however defined)," Borg writes, "the greater the number of people who did not meet them."[10] Ched Myers describes how the poor were particularly victimized by such an order:

> The major obstacles to rigorous conformity to the demands of the symbolic system for ordinary persons were economic. The daily circumstances of their lives and trades, especially for the peasantry, continually exposed them to contagion, and they simply could not afford the outlay of either time or money/goods involved in ritual cleansing processes.[11]

This system had little or no room for compassion. It created a large group of "sinners" and outcasts, those who for one reason or another could not live up to the standards of the holiness code as defined by religious leaders and tradition. It is, of course, to these marginalized groups that Jesus comes as good news. However, this good news to the poor leads to deadly conflict with religious leaders who oversee the dominant economic and symbolic order.

Mark wastes no time in identifying the groups most responsible for the exploitation of the poor. In chapter one, verse one, as I described earlier, he poses an irreconcilable conflict between authentic gospel and empire. By verse 21 of the first chapter Jesus confronts the other pillar of the unjust system: the religious leaders who administer and benefit from the Temple-based economy and symbolic order. Together these groups become the principal adversaries of the liberating gospel.

The conflict with religious authorities finds expression the first time Jesus enters a sacred place (synagogue) at a sacred time (the Sabbath). Jesus, in this encounter, symbolically evicts the religious authorities from the synagogue:

And they went into Capernaum; and immediately on the sabbath he entered the synagogue and taught. And they were astonished at his teaching, for he taught them as one who had authority, and not as the scribes. And immediately there was in their synagogue a man with an unclean spirit; and he cried out, "What have you to do with us, Jesus of Nazareth? Have you come to destroy us? I know who you are, the Holy One of God." But Jesus rebuked him, saying, "Be silent, and come out of him." And the unclean spirit, convulsing him and crying a loud voice, came out of him. And they were all amazed ... saying, "What is this? A new teaching! With authority he commands even the unclean spirits, and they obey him" (Mk 1:21-27).

This exorcism, as in the case of the Gerasene demoniac, is deeply disturbing to the dominant order. Ched Myers writes:

> However we may view it, the possibility of manipulating the physical or spirit world was never questioned in antiquity. Nevertheless, the miracle stories of Mark go to great lengths to discourage the reader from drawing the conclusion from these stories that Jesus is a mere popular magician. Instead, the meaning of the powerful act must be found by viewing it in terms of symbolic reproduction of social conflict. ... The demon in the synagogue becomes the representative of the scribal establishment, whose "authority" undergirds the dominant Jewish social order. Exorcism represents an act of confrontation in the war of myths in which Jesus asserts his alternative authority.[12]

Throughout Mark's gospel Jesus challenges the authority of religious leaders and the legitimacy of the oppressive Temple-based economy and symbolic order they oversee. He heals a leper by touching him (1:41) and a blind man with his spit (8:23), both clear violations of purity codes; he eats with tax-collectors and sinners (those who are treated as outcasts because they violate the politics of holiness), which indicates acceptance of his table companions (2:15); and, in a direct act of civil disobedience, he heals a man with a withered hand on the Sabbath (3:1).

Jesus condemns religious authorities who exploit the poor in defense of a self-serving dominant order. *We* may domesticate the gospel to the point that we miss it, but this radical challenge was perfectly clear to these leaders. After the exorcism in the synagogue and several healing episodes they began plotting with the Herodians to murder Jesus (3:6).

There are several reasons why healing is offensive to Jesus' opponents. First, the poor health and economic marginalization of the vast majority of people is a judgment against the present order dominated by Temple and Rome. It radically undermines, as does widespread hunger in our own time, the legitimacy of the political economy and the religious institutions and leaders of society. Second, healing is dangerous because it demonstrates that oppression and marginalization are not inevitable. When Jesus heals a paralytic and announces forgiveness of sins (2:10-12), he not only takes power away from the holiness brokers who control the mechanisms of forgiveness, but he unleashes an untapped reservoir of hope. This helps explain why the religious authorities are fearful of the crowds (11:18; 12:12).

Finally, healing brings to light the tragic contradiction between compassion and "holiness" that is at the heart of the synoptic gospels. Mark illustrates this contradiction in the illegal healing of the man with a withered hand (3:2) and other controversial healings involving a leper and a paralytic; in controversies over plucking grain on the sabbath (2:23) and Jesus' practice of eating with tax-collectors and sinners (Mk 2:15); and in conflicts with religious authorities such as the casting out of the unclean spirit from the Temple (1:21) and his accusation that the scribes seek honor for themselves while devouring widows' houses (12:38-40). However, the conflict between compassion and "holiness" is best illustrated in the well-known Good Samaritan parable found in Luke. In this parable a priest and a Levite pass by to the other side of the road in order to avoid an encounter with a half-dead stranger left beaten by a roadside. The conduct of these religious leaders may be reprehensible when judged in the light of compassion, but it is entirely reasonable and legal in the context of the holiness code!

Jesus was murdered because the Spirit he experienced and embodied reflected a compassionate God. The society he confronted, despite religious appearances, could not tolerate compassion. "What distinguished him [Jesus] from most of his contemporaries as well as from us, from conventional wisdom as well as from ours," writes Marcus Borg, "was his vivid sense that reality was ultimately gracious and compassionate."[13]

The conflict between compassion and the priorities and dictates of an imperial and Temple-based society were brought to light by Jesus, sometimes through provocative acts of civil disobedience. Once out into the open, this conflict required a decision. Faced with a choice between repentance and murder, the Jewish authorities chose to collaborate with the hated Romans to kill God's messenger. It is one of the tragedies of the Jesus story and our own that unjust societies in desperate need of compassion are often incapable of receiving it precisely because compassion challenges the privileges and power of those who benefit from existing inequalities. The Jewish leaders who helped orchestrate the murder of Jesus were not "especially villainous," according to Borg. "They were the established order of their society, standing at the top of their social world politically, economically, and religiously."[14]

## Alternative Community as Gospel Imperative

The formation of an alternative community is a third essential feature of Mark's gospel story. Jesus calls forth disciples early in his ministry (1:16), and he spends a great deal of time instructing them. It is possible to identify a number of key values and characteristics that Jesus sought to build into his reform movement. His alternative community stressed compassion over codes, laws, or traditions, and healing the sick and satisfying hunger over Sabbath restrictions. The new community was inclusive of men and women, Jew and Gentile. Its servant leadership styles differed markedly from the contemporary society, where power was exercised over and at the expense of others. It affirmed rights for women and children, a remarkable occurrence in the context of a patriarchal society in which women and children had almost no rights. The community embraced priorities beyond traditional family ties and substituted costly discipleship for job security, pursuit of wealth, and honor. It embraced nonviolence, shared economic resources, healed the sick, and called the rich and powerful to conversion. Most important, the community's direction, life, and purpose were rooted in discernment of the Spirit.

Community is important because discipleship is costly. It is a formidable task, beyond the scope of any individual, to challenge empires and religious authorities that oppress the poor. Jesus, of course, does not promise his followers an easy life. However, he does promise that in the midst of costly discipleship they will find that many of the things they sacrifice will be experienced more fully in community:

> Jesus said, "Truly, I say to you, there is no one who has left house or brothers or sisters or mother or father or children or lands, for my sake and for the gospel, who will not receive a hundredfold now in this time, houses and brothers and sisters and mothers and children and lands, with persecutions, and in the age to come eternal life" (Mk 10:29-30).

Community is also important because the gospel seeks to transform rather than simply condemn the old order. Transformation involves new wine and new wineskins, new values and new structures. A gospel-filled community is a vital component in shaping an authentically new order.

I will return to a discussion of the many obstacles that impeded formation of an alternative community around Jesus and the Spirit. Before doing so, however, I want to highlight a fourth challenging feature in Mark's gospel: the shattering of myths that hold an unjust society together.

## Competing Spirits: Overcoming Destructive Myths

Oppression, according to Jesus, is not simply a product of domination by foreign troops and local collaborators; it is a consequence of the ideas and religious tenets that comprise the ideological foundation of the symbolic order. Throughout

Mark's gospel we see a struggle between competing spirits over hearts and minds. This conflict gets played out on and between different planes of reality.

Jesus, in Borg's terminology, challenges the "conventional wisdom" of his society. In Myers' language he engages his adversaries in a "war of myths." Elements of the conventional wisdom or dominant mythology included such things as God's absolute ties to the Temple and thus its invincibility, the promise of God's intervention to restore the independence of Israel, the existence of a divinely sanctioned order in which the rich are blessed and the poor and sick are sinful, and the firm belief in the viability of the holiness code. Jesus challenges these and other myths that captivate the people, result in oppression of the poor, and block the possibility of an alternative future.

Jesus, as I described earlier, confronts the symbolic order through bold acts of civil disobedience and other highly charged encounters involving healing and exorcisms. He also uses parables as a form of subversive discourse in the "war of myths" against conventional wisdom. He portrays the obstacles and possibilities of discipleship in a parable about seeds that fail to grow along a path or on rocky soil but which flourish in good soil (4:3f.); he inspires hope, faith, and resistance through stories about the smallest of all seeds growing into the greatest of all shrubs (4:30) and of seeds that grow without the knowledge of the sower (4:26); he indicates that he will oust the religious authorities from the Temple in a parable about binding a strong man (4:27); and he tells a parable about tenants of a vineyard repeatedly killing the messengers sent by the vineyard's owner, a thinly veiled attack against religious leaders who are plotting the murder of Jesus and who throughout history have murdered the prophets in defense of their own privileges (12:1-12).

These provocative challenges to the dominating order raise questions of authority throughout Mark's gospel. Jesus teaches with authority, not as the scribes (1:22); the scribes question Jesus' authority to forgive sins, and he proclaims his authority to do so as he heals the paralytic (2:7-12); and after turning over the tables in the Temple "the chief priests and the scribes and the elders came to him, and they said to him, 'By what authority are you doing these things, or who gave you this authority to do them?' " (11:27-28).

Jesus bases his authority on proper discernment of God's Spirit. In Mark, Jesus is portrayed as a Spirit-filled person, and the conflict between competing spirits is at the center of his gospel story. The Spirit drives Jesus into the wilderness immediately after his baptism. There he is tempted by an adversarial spirit, Satan, and the angels minister to him (1:12-13). Jesus casts out the unclean spirit from the synagogue (1:26). The unclean spirit, as we have seen, symbolizes religious leaders. It also explains why these authorities are ousted from the synagogue: they are serving a spirit that is not from God and therefore have no authority to teach or to lead. Jesus' adversaries accuse him of being possessed by Satan (3:4), and he responds to their accusation by warning that the only unforgivable sin is blasphemy against the Holy Spirit (3:29).

There is obviously a deeply spiritual dimension to the struggle over competing gospels. The seriousness of this conflict is illustrated by Mark's placing the temptation story immediately after Jesus' baptism and heavenly affirmation ("You are my Son, the beloved") and immediately before the arrest of John. The spirit giving shape to the dominant order is powerful and seductive; resisting that spirit is risky and costly. This is also illustrated in Luke's account of the temptation narrative (4:1-13). Jesus is led by the Spirit into the wilderness where he is tempted by the devil. The devil promises him power, authority, and glory. Clinging to the Spirit and the sovereignty of God, Jesus rejects these temptations. In the scene immediately following Jesus returns "in the power of the Spirit to Galilee" clear about his mission: He announces his ministry as good news to the poor, release to the captives, and liberty to the oppressed (4:14-21).

A key element in the "war of myths" or the struggle against conventional wisdom is discernment of the Spirit. It is Jesus, seeking and sought by the Spirit, who embodies God's will and thereby challenges an unjust order. He accuses others of being out of touch with the Spirit: they know how to interpret the weather but do not know how to interpret the present time or *kairos* (Lk 12:56); they know about Sabbath rules but have lost touch with the Spirit behind Sabbath, which is compassion (Mk

2:24-28); they thrive on religious appearances, love their privileges but oppress the poor (Mk 12:38-40).

The failure to properly discern the Spirit is costly. It leads to the murder of Jesus, the ongoing oppression of the poor, and the destruction of Jerusalem. Jesus, of course, did not come to announce the destruction of the Temple or the destruction of Jerusalem; he came to offer a choice and to warn his people of the tragic consequences of continuing their present direction. Bill Wylie Kellermann writes:

> Something has to give, and will. Jesus reads the signs of the times. He can see the suffering and the tension in the air. . . . He can see the general drift—empire, the sell-out of collaboration, revolt simmering in the countryside—but the judgment of destruction is not fixed and final. Between the corruption of the Temple City and the violence of insurrection lies hidden an alternative, a choice it is time to make: the city can see, know, choose, and change. It is a *kairos* moment of spiritual and historical opportunity. He has come to name the moment, define the choice, and provoke it with utter clarity. He is the very incarnation of the choice.[15]

The consequences of failing to discern the *kairos* are depicted in each of the gospel accounts. "And when he drew near and saw the city he wept over it, saying, 'Would that even today you knew the things that make for peace! But now they are hid from your eyes . . . you did not know the time (*kairos*) of your visitation' " (Lk 19:41, 44b).

## Obstacles to Discipleship

Mark's portrayal of the disciples is almost entirely negative. To their credit, they boldly leave families and jobs in order to respond to Jesus' call to discipleship (1:16-20). It is pretty much downhill from there. The disciples are generally deaf, dumb, and blind when it comes to understanding Jesus. Jesus teaches and embodies compassion and economic sharing; the disciples try to send the hungry crowd away (6:35). He models a new style of servant leadership; they argue among themselves about who is the greatest (9:34). Jesus affirms the rights and dignity of women and children; the disciples rebuke those who bring children to him (10:13) and reproach the woman who is bold enough to accept Jesus' death as the consequence of his faithful encounter with the powers (14:5). Jesus proclaims wealth an obstacle to the kingdom, thereby reversing conventional wisdom; his disciples, still captivated by the prevailing mythology of the dominant order, are left utterly "amazed" and "exceedingly astonished" (10:24 and 26). Jesus declares that the Temple is irreformable and will be destroyed; his disciples remain enamored with the Temple and respond, "Look, Teacher, what wonderful stones and what wonderful buildings" (13:1). Jesus embraces the way of the cross; the disciples jockey for positions of power and honor (10:36). Finally, while Jesus confronts the reality of his betrayal and murder, Peter first denies the possibility (8:32), then talks boldly of his own courage and commitment (14:28), and then denies knowing Jesus (14:68). The disciples not only can't stay awake during their leader's ordeal in Gethsemane (14:41), they are nowhere near the site of Jesus' execution. Only the women witness his ordeal (15:40).

The principal obstacles to faithful discipleship among Jesus' followers were his teaching on the Temple and the stumbling block of the cross. The Temple, as I described earlier, was the center of political, economic, and religious life. The destruction of the Temple, for the people of ancient Israel, meant the end of the world. Temple, God, and faith were inseparable. Jesus, for all the reasons cited above, proclaimed that the Temple could no longer be reformed, and he predicted its destruction. This was shocking to nearly all faithful Jews, who, regardless of their differences, remained committed to the Temple. The fact that the disciples couldn't imagine a world without the Temple demonstrates the captivating power of the symbolic order. The holiness code was deeply ingrained in the hearts and minds of the people in first-century Palestine, even among its victims.

The cross was the second stumbling block to discipleship. It symbolized the power of Rome and the weakness of the colonized. The cross pointed out how costly, and seemingly futile, discipleship really was. The disciples could accept that following

Jesus meant confrontation with the powers, but they could not accept suffering as a consequence of that confrontation. Mark and Jesus stress that in the context of fidelity to the gospel suffering and the cross do not negate the kingdom. This was particularly incomprehensible in a culture where the primary messianic expectation was triumphalistic: God was expected to lift up a leader and intervene directly in order to reestablish a kingdom independent of foreign domination. A messiah that suffered was unthinkable for Peter (8:33), for Jesus' opponents, and for the crowds who were intrigued by Jesus' ministry until his arrest and trial.

Suffering as a *consequence* of faithful discipleship is only one aspect of why the cross was problematic for the followers of Jesus. Jesus and Mark go further. They insist that the cross is also the *means* to the kingdom. It is the cross that defeats the powers! The ultimate power of all empires, including Rome, is the power to kill one's opponents. Jesus, by refusing to be silenced or intimidated by this threat, undermines this power. "By redefining the cross as the way to liberation rather than symbol of defeat and shame," Myers writes, "Mark radically subverts the authority of the empire."[16]

This understanding of cross as both the consequence and means of kingdom discipleship explains Jesus' commitment to nonviolence. Jesus and Mark, although sympathetic to those who used violence against the Roman authorities and their Jewish collaborators, insist that attempts to defeat the powers while employing violent means would only recycle oppressive power. Ched Myers writes:

> Mark realized that the problem was much deeper than throwing off the yoke of yet another colonizer. After all, biblical history itself attested to the fact that ... [earlier revolts] had only resulted in recycling oppressive power into the hands of a native dynasty. ... Thus the meaning of Jesus' struggle against the strong man is not reducible solely to his desire for the liberation of Palestine from colonial rule, though it certainly includes that. It is a struggle against the root "spirit" and politics of domination.

Myers notes that according to Mark "both parties of the colonial condominium," Roman and Jewish authorities, "are 'possessed' by this spirit, and so [Mark] assesses each in exactly the same terms." This "is reflected at the outset in the parallelism between two inaugural exorcisms, and again at the story's end in the double trial of Jesus."[17]

Apocalyptic events at three critical moments in Mark's narrative offer would-be disciples assurance that, despite appearances, God is working to establish a new kingdom through Jesus. The first event is very early in the story. Jesus, immediately before the arrest of John and after his own baptism, hears a voice from heaven: "You are my Son, the Beloved; with you I am well pleased" (1:11).

The second apocalyptic moment occurs near the midpoint of the story in an event commonly known as the transfiguration. Jesus, accompanied by several disciples, appears with Elijah and Moses on a mountain. This gathering of prophets occurs immediately after Jesus teaches his disciples that he will "be rejected by the elders and the chief priests and the scribes, and be killed" (8:31). The transfiguration functions in Mark's gospel to affirm that the cross will defeat the powers.[18] The disciples completely miss the point and propose building a shrine to commemorate the event: "Let us make three booths, one for you and one for Moses and one for Elijah" (9:5). They want worship to replace rather than reflect discipleship. The commemoration of Martin Luther King's birthday by making it a holiday is a modern-day example of a similar phenomenon. Although appropriate and symbolically important, it is also dangerous because this "national shrine" can easily substitute for authentic work to counter deep-seated racism in U.S. culture. It should be remembered that King's birthday, January 15, 1991, was the day President Bush authorized military action in the Gulf and the day he indicated his intent to release frozen funds to the Salvadoran military!

The third apocalyptic event, near the end of the story, is the tearing of the curtain at the moment of Jesus' death (15:38). This affirms that the symbolic system which anchors the unjust order has been destroyed. Together, these three heavenly signs function to affirm the call to discipleship and the way of the cross.

## Conclusion

Mark's story of Jesus, which he boldly names gospel, describes four compelling tasks of discipleship: confront the empire, challenge idolatry, form alternative community, and identify and defy destructive myths through proper discernment of the Spirit. The obstacles to following Jesus in first-century Palestine, including the stumbling blocks of costly discipleship symbolized by the cross and the inability to envision faith apart from the Temple, are mirrored today in our own attitudes and conduct. Nevertheless, Mark's gospel and the disciple's failures can help shape our discipleship journey as we confront the brave new world order of U.S. policy makers and its underlying spirit, which is violence.

CHAPTER 9

# The Church, the Gulf War, and

## the New World Order

*Here we were not only winning this war, but we were routing the enemy. . . . And yet our casualties were practically non-existent. You know, that kind of made you feel that God was on your side—had to be on your side for that to happen.*
　　　　　　　　　　　　　　—General Norman Schwarzkopf
　　　　　　　　　　　　　　*Star Tribune,* April 5, 1991

*In the churches the pastors preached devotion to flag and country and invoked the God of Battles, beseeching His aid in our good cause in outpouring of fervid eloquence which moved every listener. It was indeed a glad time, and the half-dozen rash spirits that ventured to disapprove of the war and cast a doubt upon its righteousness straightway got such a stern and angry warning that for their personal safety's sake they quickly shrank out of sight and offended no more in that way. . . . Then came the "long" prayer. None could remember the like of it for passionate pleading and moving and beautiful language. The burden of supplication was that an ever-merciful and benignant Father of us all would watch over our noble young soldiers and aid, comfort, and encourage them in their patriotic work; bless them, shield them in the day of battle and the hour of peril, bear them in His mighty hand,*

**133**

*make them strong and confident, invincible in the bloody
onset; help them to crush the foe, grant to them and to their
flag and country imperishable honor and glory—.*

—Mark Twain
*The War Poem*

We are living in a decisive moment in history. The essence
of this moment is captured in the Greek word *kairos*, a word
used by Mark and throughout the Christian Scriptures to
describe a time of opportunity within crisis. At the center of
*kairos* is a confessional crisis: Do we properly discern God's
Spirit and accept a call to discipleship rooted in the gospel of
Jesus Christ, or do we go chasing after other gods such as wealth,
power, security, and nationalism.

The most disturbing analogy between the Gulf War and Nazi
Germany isn't, as President Bush and others suggest, between
Saddam Hussein and Hitler. It is the striking parallel between
the blind patriotism of the German people and the idolatrous
patriotism that swept through our country and our churches.
Signs of idolatry were evident throughout the war, from "Desert
Shield" to "Desert Storm" to "Desert Prayer." President Bush
was accompanied by Reverend Billy Graham on the eve of his
decision to launch offensive military action in the Gulf; yellow
ribbons filled local churches; and General Schwarzkopf
expressed a common view that the outcome of the war was a
sign of God's intent for and blessing of U.S. policies. Perhaps
most disturbing was President Bush's manipulation and invo-
cation of God throughout the war and the churches' genuine
failure to challenge his assertion that the war in the Gulf was a
"just war." In his speech before the Annual Convention of
National Religious Broadcasters on January 28, 1991, Bush said:

Let me begin by congratulating you on your theme of
declaring His glory to all nations. ... While God can live
without man, man cannot live without God. His love and
His justice inspire in us a yearning for faith and a compassion for the weak and oppressed, as well as the courage
and conviction to oppose tyranny and injustice. ...
Abroad, as in America, our task is to serve and seek wisely

through the policies we pursue. Nowhere is this more true than in the Persian Gulf. . . . The war in the Gulf is not a Christian war, a Jewish war, or a Moslem war; it is a just war. And it is a war with which good will prevail. We're told that the principles of a just war originated with classical Greek and Roman philosophers. . . . And later they were expounded by such Christian theologians as Ambrose, Augustine, Thomas Aquinas. The first principle of a just war is that it support a just cause. Our cause could not be more noble. . . . But a just war must also be declared by legitimate authority. Operation Desert Storm is supported by unprecedented United Nations solidarity. . . . A just war must be a last resort. As I have often said, we did not want war. But you all know the verse from Ecclesiastes — there is "a time for peace, a time for war." . . . From the very first day of the war, the allies have waged war against Saddam's military. We are doing everything possible, believe me, to avoid hurting the innocent. Saddam's response: wanton, barbaric bombing of civilian areas. America and her allies value life. We pray that Saddam Hussein will see reason. . . . We will prevail because of the support of the American people, armed with a trust in God and in the principles that make men free — people like each of you in this room. I salute Voice of Hope's live radio programming for U.S. and allied troops in the Gulf, and your Operation Desert Prayer, and worship services for our troops held by, among others, the man who over a week ago led a wonderful prayer service at Fort Myer over here across the river in Virginia, the Reverend Billy Graham. America has always been a religious nation, perhaps never more so than now. . . . But with the support and prayers of so many, there can be no question in the minds of our soldiers or in the minds of our enemy about what Americans think. We know that this is a just war. And we know that, God willing, this is a war we will win . . . I believe more than ever that one cannot be America's president without trust in God. I cannot imagine a world, a life, without the presence of the One through whom all things are possible. . . . Thank you for this occasion. And

may God bless our great country. And please remember
all of our coalition's armed forces in your prayers. Thank
you, and God bless you.

A central feature of the new world order is that U.S. political
leaders are actively seeking and claiming religious legitimacy for
an aggressive U.S. military role in the post–Cold War period.
However, the new world order shaped by the Gulf War undermines the values and priorities of Jesus and the kingdom. Religious complicity with such an order points to a dramatic faith
crisis in which idolatry undermines the integrity of faith. We
cannot claim to be followers of Jesus unless overcoming oppression and ensuring the survival of the earth are central issues in
our lives. A faithful response to the new world order requires
Christians to break radically from the normative values, priorities, and institutions of our society. This chapter lifts up the
possibility of an authentic new world order that reflects Jesus'
vision and values, and it offers suggestions on how people of
faith, joining together in small communities, can creatively withdraw from, confront, and transform the dominating culture.

## The Church and the Gulf War

It was the best of times. It was the worst of times. Mostly it
was the worst of times, or so it seems in judging the conduct of
the churches in light of the Gulf War. On the positive side,
national leaders from numerous denominations and religious
orders opposed the war before, during and after the actual outbreak of hostilities. On the negative side, these leaders often
failed to take their protests far enough. Churches at the com-
munity-based level, particularly white churches, largely ignored
them.

In December 1990 eighteen U.S. church leaders, including
the presiding bishops of the Episcopal Church and Evangelical
Lutheran Church in America (ELCA), the General Secretary-
elect and the President of the National Council of Churches,
the President of the United Church of Christ, the General-Sec-
retary of the American Baptist Churches in the USA, and
others, warned that "we are marching toward war. ... Our

Christmas pilgrimage to the Middle East has utterly convinced us that war is not the answer. We believe the resort to massive violence to resolve the Gulf crisis would be politically and morally indefensible."[1]

Edgar Trexler, editor of *The Lutheran*, in an editorial written just days before the U.S. air war began, noted that a war in the Gulf could not meet "just war" criteria. "From a Christian ethics stance," he wrote, "this war wouldn't be justifiable."[2]

National church leaders continued their opposition even after the outbreak of hostilities and as support for the war began building among the general U.S. population. On January 22, 1991, a week into the fighting, Joan Chittister, a Catholic sister and director of the Alliance for International Monasticism, spoke against the war on behalf of twenty-one heads of religious communities and thirty-nine representatives of other religious orders. "We are not here as religious leaders because we are unpatriotic but because we are patriotic enough to protest what is clearly an anti-American war being waged by us and against our own democratic principles. Unless we live up to our own ideals," she noted, "we will soon find that we have lost them, and, under those conditions, people under God cannot, must not, and will not be silent."[3]

On Ash Wednesday, February 13, 1991, "A Call to the Churches" was issued by church leaders expressing their continued opposition to the war. Signed by leaders of more than twenty Protestant and Orthodox denominations—including five historic black churches, fifteen Roman Catholic bishops, dozens of Catholic women's and men's orders, evangelical groups, and a variety of ecumenical organizations and movements—it noted that "the churches were at the forefront of those urging peaceful alternatives to war in the Middle East." As fighting took a deadly toll they called for "a fresh effort to find a diplomatic solution." They said that they "opposed this war on moral grounds and remain opposed to it now."[4]

The degree of opposition to the Gulf War expressed by national church leaders is unprecedented in U.S. history. It is a hopeful sign in the midst of a deepening religious and political crisis. Unfortunately, apart from these efforts, the conduct of the churches during the Gulf War is profoundly disturbing. This is true because local congregations throughout the country generally embraced the Gulf War and because, given the severity of the crisis, national church leaders could have done more to sharpen the conflict between church and state and to expose idolatry within the churches, before, during, and after the war.

Local religious support for the war was the result of a combination of factors, including concern about the well-being of congregational members or their families who were sent to the Gulf, the success of propaganda efforts to demonize Saddam Hussein and to present U.S. actions as moral imperatives, and a long-standing problem of churches being too closely identified with the dominating culture. The war revealed how thoroughly the "gospel" had reverted to its earlier meaning of imperial conquest and how patriotism, affluence, and power had displaced Jesus as the functional lords in the lives of most parishioners and churches.

There were exceptions to the pattern of grass-roots church support for the Gulf War. Most notably, African-American pastors and political activists took leadership in opposing the Gulf War in many communities around the country. On February 15, 1991, more than one hundred black leaders from across the nation attended a National Emergency African-American Leadership Summit on the Gulf War at Abyssinian Baptist Church in Harlem. In an open letter to President Bush summit participants wrote:

The war in the Gulf is wrong, unnecessary, unprincipled, and dirty. . . . The United States is spending $1 billion a day to wage war when we should be spending that much and more to wage peace, educate all our youth, cure all our diseases, unshackle all our alcoholics and dope addicts, train all our workers, employ all our people, provide housing and food for all our families and liberate all our oppressed. It is troubling to realize that the same president who fears the over-representation of blacks and other minorities in American jobs, corporate positions and academic institutions, does not object to over-representation of blacks and other minorities on the front lines of battle. Mr. President, you refused to support any approximation of affirmative action, refused to sign the Civil Rights Bill of 1990, refused to maintain the legality of minority scholarships; but you voice no objection to the fact that blacks and other minorities are over-represented in the military and are dying disproportionately in the present war.[5]

Similar criticisms were expressed by other African-American leaders. Coretta Scott King noted that war is not "an equal opportunity destroyer" and that "conditions of social and economic injustice ... force African-American youths to seek escape in the military."[6] Reverend Benjamin F. Chavis, Jr., executive director of the Commission for Racial Justice for the United Church of Christ said that Christians "must demand a change in national priorities, from huge military expenditures to meaningful programs to eliminate poverty and social injustice."[7] And according to Anthony Parker:

The cost of one day of fighting in the Gulf could increase by five times the amount spent last year ($200 million) on emergency food and shelter for the homeless; two days of war could pay for the entire annual cost of the Head Start program ($1.9 billion) or the Women, Infants, and Children (WIC) program and spending on health care ($1.4 billion); and five days of war could pay for the entire annual cost of our child nutrition program ($4.8 billion).[8]

Parker notes that despite significant opposition to the Gulf War within the African-American community there was a profound "crisis of vision and leadership" evident in its posture toward the Gulf War. The war illustrated the failure of "black integrationist political philosophy." There was little or no likelihood, he pointed out, that the priorities of the Bush administration would address the needs of African Americans with or without the Gulf War. He also noted that "no black politician or religious leader has dared to challenge Powell's [General Colin Powell, Chair of the Joint Chiefs of Staff, is black] politics or question his role as chief military architect of the war in the Persian Gulf and the invasion of Panama. And they won't," he continued, "because they live in glass houses."

The moral imperative for blacks right now is to ask ourselves how we can challenge an unjust war in the Persian Gulf when so many of us are dependent upon its success militarily, politically, and economically. What purpose does it serve for our churches to offer sanctuary to black conscientious objectors when our black colleges are prime recruiting areas for ROTC? If the United States' foreign policy is immoral, and if our armed forces are instrumental in carrying out that foreign policy, shouldn't we counsel blacks not to enter the military?[9]

The lack of vision and leadership noted by Parker in the African-American community is much more pronounced among grass-roots white churches, which remain subservient to the dominating culture and to the ideology and political objectives of the National Security State Establishment.

Another reason for a negative assessment of the churches' response to the Gulf War is that church leaders, who took significant risks in opposing what became the most popular war in U.S. history, failed to follow their conviction to its logical conclusion. The Gulf War, they said throughout, could not meet just-war criteria and was potentially catastrophic—politically, militarily, and environmentally. In this context the churches needed to speak a clear word to elevate the clash between religious faith and the dominant U.S. society. Opponents of the Gulf War, including those in the religious community, were often sidetracked by a debate about who did and did not support the troops. This should never have been an issue. The church's obligation was to inform soldiers and parishioners alike that *they had no moral legitimacy to fight in or pay for an unjust war.*

Bishop Thomas Gumbleton of Detroit was perhaps alone among U.S. church leaders in calling on soldiers to refuse to fight in the unjust Gulf War.[10] Edgar Trexler came close to a clear, faith-based position in his editorial in *The Lutheran.* He cited Luther: "If a prince desired to go to war and his cause was clearly unrighteous, we should neither follow nor help such a prince."[11] However, he failed to make explicit what this might mean in the context of the Gulf War.

A faith-based stance calling for noncooperation with an

unjust war may have cost many pastors and church leaders their jobs. However, it could have forced a meaningful national debate about the Gulf War and the imperatives of a National Security State as well as dramatically called into question the idolatrous patriotism infecting many churches. It would have been infinitely preferable to criticism of U.S. policy that limited the moral imperative for bold action. For example, "A Call to the Churches," referred to earlier, is a positive statement, but it offers a smorgasbord of options that undermines the urgency of its message:

> Let our churches exercise their pastoral and prophetic ministry by becoming places of comfort and calm sanctuary. . . . Let our churches be havens of prayer, silence, and meditation. . . . Let our churches offer prayers of intercession for wisdom and compassion on the part of political leaders on all sides of this conflict. . . . Let our churches provide pastoral support for military personnel. . . . Let our churches stand ready to help those returning from war. . . . Let our churches offer support and assistance to conscientious objectors. . . . Let our churches become places for reasoned discussion and spiritual discernment. . . . Let our churches speak clearly their historic teaching on war and peace. . . . Let our churches give voice to the cries for justice. . . . Let our churches embrace the bereaved, maimed and homeless. . . . Let our churches become centers for nonviolence. . . . Let Christians help build a disciplined, morally based nonviolent movement in response to the Gulf and in response to poverty and suffering throughout the world.[12]

In sum, at one of the most critical moments in world history the response of many church leaders was inadequate and the response of many local churches idolatrous. The U.S. National Security Establishment successfully manipulated a crisis, foreclosed on the peace dividend, and created a new world order based on U.S. military supremacy. It did so in the context of significant but inadequate protests from national church leaders and full support or minimal resistance from local churches. As a result, the future became more precarious for U.S. democracy, the church, U.S. and third-world poor, and the earth itself. The religious significance of the Gulf War is that the church, with a few notable exceptions, has become captive to the dominant values and ideology of the U.S. National Security State Establishment.

## A Gospel-Informed Agenda

The context of our discipleship journey is a new world order marred by religious complicity with militarism, hunger, and environmental decay. Before outlining elements of a faithful response to such an order, it might be helpful to review some key aspects of the analysis to this point:

• In the aftermath of the Cold War powerful groups are shaping a new world order that deepens the injustice of the old order.

• The third-world poor are particularly vulnerable within the new world order. A world shaped around East-West power struggles is giving way to a Northern alliance against the nations of the South with the IMF and U.S. military performing key police functions.

• The U.S. poor are also victims of this new order. The needs of U.S. poor and working-class citizens are being sacrificed to the desires of elite economic and military sectors, which benefit from speculative and other forms of nonproductive investment. Also, within the new order, U.S. businesses are seeking to restore their competitive position by reducing the living standards of U.S. workers. Reducing living standards, along with sacrificing the environment, are substitutes for authentic revitalization based on improving the social and economic infrastructure of the country.

• The end of the Cold War was a momentous event in world history. It offered the United States and the world the possibility to reorient priorities in an effort to overcome poverty, to respond to environmental threats to global survival, and to shape an authentically new order based on nonviolent resolution of conflict.

•The Gulf War, seen in this light, is one of history's greatest disasters. The U.S. National Security State Establishment manipulated the Gulf War in order to foreclose on the peace dividend and establish a world order in which U.S. superpower status is at least temporarily maintained through military power. It was aided in its effort by presidential leadership, Congressional acquiescence, church complicity and involvement, and enthusiastic support from the media.

• The triumph of the U.S. National Security State not only ensures further erosion of U.S. democracy, growing domestic poverty, the economic decline of the United States, and imposition of an unjust order on third-world peoples, but it also jeopardizes the survival of the planet.

•We have approximately forty years to make a transition to sustainable societies. This transition involves overcoming poverty, changing values, transforming patterns of production and consumption, and shifting from fossil fuels to renewable energy sources. If we fail to make this transition during the prescribed period, we will have irreversibly set in motion the destruction of the earth.

• The transition to sustainable societies is possible. However, a sustainable future depends on vision, political will, and a dramatic shift of priorities away from militarism.

• There are competing gospels and competing spirits active in the world.

• Massive idolatry characterizes the role of churches and individual Christians in relation to these issues.

Mark's gospel, in light of these concerns, provides a general outline of our task as individuals, communities, and churches:

• The gospel is incompatible with empire; we are Christians living in an empire and faithful discipleship will involve efforts to confront and transform the dominant society.

• The gospel condemns religious authorities and institutions that oppress the poor; the lives of individual Christians as well as churches within the empire have become massively idolatrous. Our subservience to empire leads to hunger, poverty, and oppression. Our agenda must, therefore, include efforts to revitalize our faith.

• The gospel calls forth new values and priorities rooted in alternative community; our discipleship journey must seek to build community as a means of transforming both church and society.

• The gospel challenges the underlying spirit of the dominant mythology or symbolic order that captivates us and holds us in bondage to unjust systems; our agenda must include discernment of the Spirit and confrontation with the myths that are the ideological foundation of the new world order.

• The gospel highlights various obstacles to discipleship: the cross as consequence and means of the kingdom; a fear of costly discipleship rooted in nonviolence; and the inability to envision faith in God apart from survival of the Temple. Our agenda must include a willingness to take risks, to embrace nonviolence, and to envision new ways of being church.

Participants at the World Council of Churches convocation Justice, Peace, and the Integrity of Creation agreed to a fourfold act of covenanting around issues of vital concern to Christians committed to building an authentically new world order.

I. For a just economic order on local, national, regional and international levels for all people ... we commit ourselves to work and to engage our churches to work (1) towards economic systems and policies which reflect that people come first; (2) towards a church free of complicity with unjust economic structures ... (3) towards liberation from the bondage to foreign debts and a just structure of the international financial system.

II. For the true security of all nations and peoples, for the demilitarization of international relations, against militarism and national security doctrines and systems, for a culture of nonviolence as a force for change and liberation ... we commit ourselves to work and to engage our churches to work (1) for a community of the churches who claim their identity as the Body of Christ through providing witness to the liberating love of God; (2) for a comprehensive notion of security ... this common security has to grow from a realization of peace with justice, and includes the defense of God's creation; (3) for a halt to militarization ... ; (4) for the demilitarization of international relations and the promotion of nonviolent forms of defense; (5) for a culture of active nonviolence, life-promoting, which is not a withdrawal from situations of violence and oppression but is a way to work for justice and liberation.

III. For building a culture that can live in harmony with creation's integrity ... we commit ourselves to work and to engage our churches to work (1) to join in the search for ways to live together in harmony with God's creation; (2) to join in global, local and personal efforts to safeguard the world's atmospheric integrity and quality; (3) to resist globally the causes and deal with the consequences of atmospheric destruction; (4) to call on our churches to lead in the indispensable reversal of the thinking which supports unlimited energy consumption and economic growth; (5) to commit ourselves personally to promote and facilitate the achievement of these goals.

IV. For the eradication of racism and discrimination on national and international levels for all people, for the breaking down of walls which divide people because of their ethnic origin, for the dismantling of the economic, political and social patterns of behavior that perpetuate and allow individuals to consciously and unconsciously perpetuate the sin of racism ... we commit ourselves to work and to engage our churches to work (1) for just systems and policies which reflect that every human being is beloved of God ... (2) towards implementation of the above-mentioned principles in the policies and practices of church-related bodies.[13]

As people and communities of faith within a dominating culture, we are often captives to an imperial gospel. This precludes discipleship and undermines the possibility of an alternative future. Jesus sought to build into his movement the values and priorities of compassion, healing, satisfying hunger, overcoming patriarchy, servant leadership, sufficiency, nonviolence, inclusivity, economic sharing, costly discipleship, and discernment of the Spirit. The gap between these and the values and priorities of contemporary U.S. culture could not be wider.

The temptation is to be seduced by the dominating order or to be overwhelmed by it and therefore slip into denial or into violent retaliation against its abuses. Mark's gospel points another way. Ched Myers provides the following summary:

> Mark, a follower of Jesus, struggling and suffering through the apocalyptic moment of the late war years, responded with a story about a Nazarene and his followers. It legitimated neither defection, nor withdrawal, nor reform minded moderation, nor Maccabean triumphalism, nor despairing acceptance of a world dominated by the powers. It called for resistance to the rule of the "strong man," and the creation of a new world: a practice of radical discipleship. This story heralded a way through the wilderness—and the war. But this way was the way of the cross: to the Romans a symbol of imperial hegemony, to Mark the sign of the kingdom come.[14]

Christians are called to continue this discipleship journey. Part of our task is creatively to bring the contradictions between authentic and imperial gospels to light. I believe that our response to the brave new world order must include both efforts creatively to withdraw from the dominant society and creatively to confront it. Withdrawal without creative confrontation is escapism. Confrontation without creative withdrawal can lead to cooptation and may ultimately be futile.

The following "agenda" for people of faith seems consistent with Mark's gospel in the context of the "brave new world order."

*First, we must consciously form communities.* Community has many meanings depending on the context. Certainly we need to revitalize the communities within which we live. There is also a striking need to build a community of nations. However, I am using *community* here in the sense of small groups of committed Christians, finding one another in their neighborhoods or congregations and consciously joining together in order to deepen their faith and action.[15]

There are three vital components in the life of such communities: bible study, social analysis (examination of key local, national, and international issues), and action. These components function together, forming a continuous interactive circle that should not be broken. The purpose of bible study is to encourage discipleship, not simply to know more about Jesus; the goal of social analysis is transforming action, not simply to know more about difficult social problems. Social actions are then evaluated and reformulated in the context of further bible study and social analysis.

Our faith-based communities, like Jesus, must be provocative and confrontational. Jesus refused to shy away from necessary conflict. He challenged the idolatry of riches, overturned the tables of the moneychangers, and carried out provocative acts of civil disobedience. However, our communities, again like Jesus, must also be invitational. He invited disciples to join him, and he embodied compassion through healing, table fellowship, and economic sharing.

The emptiness of the dominating culture requires more than condemnation. It requires meaningful examples of new ways of living. In the lifestyles we embrace and in the communities we form, we must seek to be living signs of an authentically new order. Invitational communities can be a foundation from which the churches and other institutions of the dominant society can be challenged and transformed while avoiding the pitfalls of what could easily become a newly defined holiness code. Compassionate communities, in which people care about each other and creation, share resources and skills, concern themselves with healing, work to change unjust social structures, and demonstrate new leadership styles can help others envision an alternative future capable of challenging the values and priorities of the brave new world order.

The goals of overcoming oppression and restoring the ecological integrity of the earth must be at the heart of individual and community decision-making. If this were to happen, it could have a profound impact on the institutional churches and the society as a whole. Jon Sobrino says that we can't be believers in God if we do not make overcoming oppression the central issue of our lives. He also says that while the world may need more liberation theologians, what it needs first and foremost are liberation plumbers, liberation teachers, liberation doctors, liberation retirees, liberation lawyers, liberation carpenters and other people who will put their particular skills to use in overcoming oppression.[16]

The gospel beckons us to come and die. The murder of Jesus and Jesuit priests and others makes clear that death should not only be understood metaphorically. Imperial crosses function in history both to deter fidelity and to remind us of the costs of discipleship. However, dying can also be understood symbolically without robbing the gospel of its compelling claim on our lives. Baptism signifies our death to dominating systems, values, and cultures and our rebirth into communities of discipleship and compassion.

Imagine the liberating potential that exists in each of our congregations! In many cases, skilled and creative persons are wasting their gifts in pursuit of affluence and private security. Others are crippled through the internalization of oppression. They need to hear a compelling gospel word, to see a life-giving vision, to hear an urgent call, to envision a practical and authentically new possibility. Alternative communities, in and at the edge of the churches, can take leadership in revitalizing hope and calling forth and channeling peoples' gifts and skills. Such an endeavor could have a liberating impact on the individuals themselves, the people with whom they work, the communities of which they are a part, and the church and society as a whole.

*Second, as people of faith we must be willing to speak the truth to one another and to the dominant society.* We live in a culture enamored with lies, deception, and violence. Overcoming poverty and ensuring global survival depend on successfully challenging the imperial gospel and its symbolic order. The imperial gospel may have reached its zenith in the immediate aftermath of the Gulf War. U.S. military power appeared supreme and the symbolic order captivated people who lined the streets of major U.S. cities waving flags and ribbons, celebrating imperial conquest, and worshiping the weapons of destruction.

It is profoundly disturbing to remember that parades and imperial celebrations were a common feature of life for the Roman empire and the Third Reich. Jesus, Kellermann reminds us, "was killed in a Roman liturgy of political execution."[17] In his commentary on Mark, Ched Myers notes that Jesus was a victim of Rome's common practice of parading defeated foes through public streets:

> When the Roman security forces have completed the deeds of the torture-room, Jesus is marched out of the city to the place of crucifixion (15:20). The drama of the *via dolorosa*, like many aspects of the gospel narrative, has become in churchly tradition a pious exercise in personal anguish. . . . Gone is its true signification: the political theater of imperial triumph.[18]

Crucifixion was a powerful deterrent, a form of psychological warfare. Victory parades served a similar function. They both discouraged protest and buoyed the spirits of the victors. Kellermann notes the common features and the purpose of Rome's standard victory processions: Captured arms and other spoils of war, prisoners, political and military leaders, triumphant soldiers, and the latest weapons of war were paraded past the public in ceremonies designed to convey a message of "imperial omnipotence."[19]

The triumph of imperial symbols in the United States is illustrated by the fact that people are more concerned about flag burning than about the erosion of U.S. democracy. The gospel claims of powerful competing spirits vying for control of the hearts and minds of people are not mythology relegated to a distant past. There is a deep spiritual crisis behind the otherwise inexplicable scene of major U.S. cities, crippled by poverty and inequality, holding victory parades to celebrate the triumph of the National Security State and their own destruction.

Christians, faith communities, and churches must be willing to confront the symbolic order that is infected with a spirit of violence and that dresses itself in compelling myths. We must state through bold words and creative actions that the new world order isn't new; that it oppresses the poor and is rooted in violence; that the United States is an empire and not a benevolent superpower; that we do not live in a Christian nation but an idolatrous one; that God stands with the victims and not the victors of war; that the National Security State, not democracy, is the fundamental feature of U.S. political life; that undermining diplomacy in favor of militarization is reprehensible and not a moral imperative; that racism is a pervasive feature of U.S. foreign and domestic policies; that wealth is an obstacle to the kingdom, not a sign of God's blessing; that poverty is rooted in unjust social structures, not a sign of unworthiness or personal sin; that spirituality, not consumption, will satisfy our deepest longings; that it is possible to live more meaningful lives with fewer rather than more possessions; that capitalism is not an economic savior, but oppresses the poor and may destroy the planet; that faith and politics inform each other and, while they should never be equated, it is wrong to rigidly separate them; that changed values and priorities, not technological miracles, will solve the environmental crisis; that change is possible and resignation is neither prudent nor biblical.

*Third, we must take risks.* Our actions as individuals, communities, and churches must be creative, bold, practical, and symbolic. It is tempting to leave this challenge vague, as is the case with so many sermons. However, I am going to get very specific. I believe at the depth of my being that the churches' complicity with the new world order, that order's captivity to the imperial gospel, and its subservience to the imperatives of the National Security State are leading to an unnecessary disaster.

Overcoming oppression and ensuring the earth's survival depend on our willingness to reorder personal and societal priorities and to engage in actions big and small. We can recycle as we work to build an economy based on recycled materials; we can share tools, money, and talents as we organize to retool the global economy; we can hang clothes to dry and use returnable bottles while promoting alternatives to fossil-fuel-intensive energy sources; we can insulate homes and other buildings while refusing to insulate ourselves and our families from the difficult issues that threaten global survival; we can walk, use bicycles, travel by bus, and live close to our places of work while promoting new work styles and alternatives to more cars and highways; we can limit consumption and redefine success; we can share our homes with others as we work to reestablish decent housing as a national priority; we can engage in tax resistance and work for tax reform to encourage equality and environmental integrity; we can refuse military service or military-related employment while working for a national and global strategy of peace conversion; and as parents we can invest the time and patience it takes to have healthy families even as we demand a national health system that guarantees all citizens the right to adequate health care.

Faced with the imminent death of the planet and confronted with a new world order based on poverty and militarism, Christians and churches in the United States must embrace the imperative of radical discipleship. Specifically, this requires embracing and encouraging tax resistance and nonviolence. It means that individuals, communities and churches will be called on to take meaningful risks.

Alternative faith communities and churches must take leadership in a faith-based tax revolt against the economic priorities of the U.S.-led new world order and the military priorities of the National Security State. Tax resistance can be expressed in many different ways, some more effective than others: living below a taxable income; refusal to pay the federal tax on our phone bills, which functions as a war tax; withholding the percentage of our taxes that are used for military purposes; enclosing a letter of protest when filing our tax returns; delivering the equivalent of taxes owed in food stuffs to our local Internal Revenue Service (IRS) offices.

Taxes in themselves are not bad; the present use of tax dollars is. Our taxes feed distorted priorities that impoverish the poor and threaten the earth. I mentioned earlier that the word that was most needed from the church during the Gulf War was a call to Christians for noncooperation, including tax resistance and refusal to fight. This word is still needed in the aftermath of the Gulf War.

Faith communities and churches must also boldly proclaim that active nonviolence is normative for Christians. This is particularly important for Christians who live in an empire such as ours. We must refuse to serve in the U.S. military or related agencies. Those already serving should be encouraged to leave their positions immediately. The same is true for Christians employed in defense or defense-related industries. We can no longer use our labor to produce or contribute to the production of weapons. Faith communities and churches can encourage and facilitate such actions among our constituencies by delegitimizing Christian involvement in military service and production; by supporting soldiers, defense workers, and their families during a difficult transition; and by taking leadership in demanding national efforts for peace conversion. However, these steps of noncompliance cannot be postponed until a national peace conversion process is underway. They must jump-start such a process.

A faith-based commitment to nonviolence and a refusal to participate in military service and production would help us liberate ourselves and our churches from the clutches of the imperial gospel. They would also reestablish our ties to the Jesus movement, which regrouped after the crucifixion and resurrection of Jesus. "Those closest to Jesus in time clearly understood his teaching to mean nonviolence," writes Marcus Borg. "The early church for the first three hundred years of its existence was pacifist."[20]

A radical commitment to nonviolence and a refusal to serve the empire through military service would also help us reclaim the sacrament of baptism. Baptism is a powerful symbol of identity, freedom, and commitment rooted in the Spirit and in conflict with ultimate allegiances demanded by the powers. For Christians living under Roman domination, there were competing sacraments just as there were competing gospels. Sacraments had military implications and imperial significance. Bill Wylie Kellermann writes:

> *Sacrament* first meant an oath of loyalty or allegiance, in this case the oath of *military induction* sworn to the emperor, before the gods. Indeed, to be a Roman soldier entailed not only making the vow, but submitting to a liturgical cycle of religious observances officially prescribed and enforced.[21]

The early church rejected violence because it understood nonviolence to be central to Jesus and the kingdom. It refused military service because killing was incompatible with Christian faith and because a sacrament of allegiance to the empire violated the sovereignty of God and the ultimate allegiance of Christian people. Kellermann, noting the incompatibility of Christian baptism with military service, quotes Hippolytus, who describes the "prescriptive requirements of baptism" in third-century Rome:

> A soldier with authority must not kill people. If he is commanded, he must refuse, and he must not take an oath. If he will not agree, he must be rejected [not baptized]. Those who have the power of the sword, or a civil magistrate who wears the purple, must cease or be rejected. If a catechumen, or one of the faithful wishes to become a soldier, let him be rejected, for he has despised God.[22]

It is time to make nonviolence and refusal to participate in military service and military-related employment normative for Christians. It is also time to acknowledge that there is no such thing as a just war. An editorial saying just that appeared in the July 6, 1991 issue of *La Civilta Catolica* which, according to a *National Catholic Reporter* article, "reflects Vatican thinking." The editorial states that "war is always immoral," the conditions of a just war "were and are unattainable" and the Gulf War shows that modern wars are "irrational."[23] Other similar actions are important in the "war of myths" against the spirit of the symbolic order that shapes the dominating U.S. culture. I believe that Christians should remove flags from all churches and refuse to pledge allegiance to the flag of any nation-state, including our own. Flags and pledges of allegiance violate our fundamental allegiance to a sovereign God. The first commandment of the Hebrew Bible is to have no other gods, and the early Christians were murdered because they insisted that Jesus, not Caesar, is Lord.

The most difficult problem confronting churches, pastors, and church leaders is this: Fidelity to the gospel in the context of the brave new world order involves new ways of being church. The destruction of the Temple in first-century Palestine meant the end of the world for many Jews. The end of our world could take a variety of forms: the end of U.S. superpower status; the end of innocence as we unmask the symbolic order of our unjust society; the end of an auto-centered culture and economy; or the end of the world through ecological destruction. It might also mean the end of the church in its present form.

A deep impulse throughout history, including in our present moment, is for the church to preserve the institution at the expense of fidelity to the gospel. Like the disciples who witnessed the transfiguration, we want to build a shrine and substitute worship for discipleship. Building or maintaining a shrine isn't risky. Discipleship is. Risk-free Christianity should be called by some other name. It is faith lived at the least common denominator.

The church, with few exceptions, is good at building shrines and poor at discipleship. This is illustrated by the numbers of elaborate churches that dot our country and the relative ease with which many carry out successful building drives and expansion programs. During the years that I coordinated the hunger taskforce for a Lutheran synod I was always struck by the contrast between money spent on buildings and that spent to combat hunger. Giving to a well-run national hunger program designed to meet emergency needs, foster long-term development, and address root causes was only approximately three dollars per confirmed member per year.

The point here is that in the context of a new world order that serves the interests of the National Security State while victimizing the poor and threatening environmental catastrophe, it is a gospel imperative for the church to assume a more prophetic role. There are enormous pressures—financial, cultural, and political—that impede the church from doing so. Breaking with the imperial gospel will take faith and courage. It may destroy the church as we now know it. I am a life-long Lutheran. I am part of an alternative faith community, the Community of St. Martin, am active in my local congregation, participate in the local synod, and am involved with my national church. In sum, I am committed to the church and do not seek its destruction. However, I believe if a desire to maintain the institutional church in its present form prevents it from taking bold risks, then the church will have been deaf to God's Spirit and missed its opportunity within crisis at a decisive moment in world history. I also believe that if the church were "destroyed" or torn apart in the context of faithful discipleship that it would not be an end but a new beginning for the church. The discipleship journey would continue.

The church in the context of a brave new world order must call Christians to faithful action, encourage alternative community, affirm nonviolence, encourage biblically based resistance, repent, challenge and break with the dominant symbolic order, cast out unclean spirits and any vestiges of the imperial gospel that continue to distort its life, be deeply pastoral and prophetic, make overcoming poverty and planetary survival the central features of its life, link belief to discipleship, and be a living sign that it has experienced a loving and compassionate God.

## Conclusion

John also laughed, but for another reason—laughed for pure joy. "O brave new word," he repeated. "O brave new world. . . . Let's start at once."

"You have a most peculiar way of talking sometimes," said Bernard, staring at the young man in perplexed astonishment. "And anyhow, hadn't you better wait till you actually see the new world?"

We return to where we started. The brave new world that John celebrated without having seen it tormented him once he arrived. John, toward the end of Huxley's novel, is looking frightfully ill. " 'Did you eat something that didn't agree with you?' asked Bernard. [John] nodded. 'I ate civilization. . . . It poisoned me; I was defiled. And then,' he added, in a lower tone, 'I ate my own wickedness.' "[24]

The new world order, like the *Brave New World* of Huxley's novel, sounds inviting. It is uncritically embraced by many. Upon reflection and in light of experience, however, it continues to impoverish the people and threatens to destroy the earth. It should inspire resistance, not allegiance. As those who seek to follow Jesus, our goal is to be faithful in the context of a brave new world order; it is not to construct a new holiness code. Jesus invites us to pick up our crosses and come follow. The cross, as we have seen, is a consequence of faithful discipleship and a means to the kingdom. It is also at the heart of Christian understanding of atonement. Jesus, the suffering servant who teaches servant leadership to his disciples, gives his life on a cross for our sins. We are forgiven. The power of Rome and the holiness code are defeated. They can no longer bind us.

We live under a broad canopy of God's grace and compassion in a world order so void of compassion that it condemns billions of people to subhuman living conditions and threatens the earth itself. The church has too often announced God's grace and compassion, not to call forth compassion in the context of radical discipleship, but to deny the need for confrontation.

Dietrich Bonhoeffer, killed by Hitler after being implicated in an assassination plot, once said that to be a patriot in the context of Nazi Germany meant praying for the defeat of his country. I believe his difficult words are equally appropriate for us: praying and working for the defeat of our country in the context of its goals and priorities within the new world order is a gospel imperative.

The new world order is filled with contradictions. In the months and years ahead the conflict between global survival and the priorities of the National Security State Establishment will intensify. Euphoria for the Gulf War will diminish as the problems of poverty and environmental decay deepen within our own country and throughout the world. Cracks will appear and then widen, exposing once hidden flaws in the symbolic order. Captivity may give way to resistance. Ironically, our present moment, so filled with reasons for despair, is also a time ripe for building a social change movement capable of leading us into the next century with overcoming poverty and the survival of the planet as key goals.

People of faith have much to contribute in this time of opportunity within crisis. If we can allow the gospel of Jesus Christ to free us from the shackles of the imperial gospel then we can change our own lives, build alternative communities, and revitalize our churches. As gospel-led people, discerning of the

Spirit and committed to discipleship, we can creatively confront and seek to transform our society.

One of the most powerful features of Mark's gospel narrative is how he ends the story. Triumphalistic endings have been added by later writers. However, Mark's ending is both disturbing and powerful. Jesus has been crucified and his body placed in a tomb. Several women go to anoint his body but find the stone removed and his body missing. They are greeted by a young man, clothed in the linen of martyrs, who tells them:

> "Do not be amazed; you seek Jesus of Nazareth, who was crucified. He has risen, he is not here; see the place where they laid him. But go, tell his disciples, and Peter that he is going before you to Galilee; there you will see him, as he told you." And they went out and fled from the tomb; for trembling and astonishment had come upon them; and they said nothing to any one, for they were afraid (Mk 16:6-8).

The tasks which lie before us are formidable. However, we need not be depressed; we should not look for Jesus in a tomb. The disciples, who bungled their way through Mark's gospel, regrouped. The power of the resurrection claimed their lives, and the discipleship journey continued with the guidance of the Holy Spirit.

Like the women at the end of Mark's gospel, we are undoubtedly afraid. However, we can overcome our fear and refuse to be silent because for those of us who "seek Jesus of Nazareth, who was crucified" the news is good indeed. The powers have been defeated. "He has risen!" Mark ends his story by inviting us in. We continue the discipleship journey. The promise of the gospel is that Jesus meets with us on the way.

# Notes

---

### Introduction

1. "War Is Not the Answer," *Sojourners* (February-March 1991), p. 5.

2. *Star Tribune*, 25 February 1991.

3. George Bush, "Address Before a Joint Session of the Congress on the State of the Union," 29 January 1991. Quotations from President Bush in the Introduction are from this address unless otherwise noted.

4. This letter was dated 28 November 1989, several days after the murder of two women and six Jesuit priests at the Catholic University in El Salvador. It was addressed to Mr. George Bush, President of the United States of America, Secretary of State, Members of Congress, [and] Leaders of the Christian Churches and of the Religious and Humanitarian Organizations in the United States.

5. George Bush, "Message to Allied Nations on the Persian Gulf Crisis," 8 January 1991.

6. George Bush, "Radio Address to the Nation on the Persian Gulf Crisis," 5 January 1991.

7. "Burned Stories from Media Gulf," by Holly Sklar, *Z Magazine* (March 1991), p. 59.

8. Lester R. Brown, et al., *State of the World 1990* and *State of the World 1991* (New York: W. W. Norton, 1990 and 1991).

### Chapter 1

1. Joel Beinin, "Origins of the Gulf War," a talk given at the University of Wisconsin in Madison on 30 November 1990.

2. Ibid.

3. *Z Magazine* (February 1991), p. 50.

4. *A Children's Defense Budget, FY 1989: An Analysis of Our Nation's Investment in Children* (Washington, D.C.: Children's Defense Fund, 1988).

5. Pablo Richard, "The 1990s: A Hope for the Third World," in *Total War Against the Poor* (New York: New York Circus Publications, 1990), p. 201.

6. Dr. Norman Meyers, ed., *GAIA: An Atlas of Planet Management* (New York: Anchor Press/Doubleday & Company, 1984). See also, Ulrich Duchrow, *Global Economy: A Confessional Issue for the Churches?* (Geneva: WCC Publications, 1987).

7. *Sojourners* (February-March 1990), p. 5.

8. Noam Chomsky, "The Victors: III," *Z Magazine* (April 1991), pp. 43-44.

9. For a detailed analysis of the strategy of U.S. interventionism in the Third World, see Jack Nelson-Pallmeyer, *War Against the Poor: Low-Intensity Conflict and Christian Faith* (Maryknoll, NY: Orbis Books, 1989).

10. World Bank, *The Assault on Poverty: Problems of Rural Development, Education, and Health* (Baltimore: Johns Hopkins University Press, 1975), pp. 215-16.

11. Ecumenical Coalition for Economic Justice, *Recolonization or Liberation: The Bonds of Structural Adjustment and Struggles for Emancipation* (Toronto: Ecumenical Coalition for Economic Justice, 1990), p. 6.

12. Michael Harrington, *Socialism Past and Future* (New York: Arcade Publishing, 1989), p. 247.

13. Walden Bello, *Brave New Third World? Strategies for Survival in the Global Economy* (San Francisco: The Institute for Food and Development Policy, 1989), p. 64.

14. *Recolonization or Liberation*, p. 19.

15. Ibid.

16. Ibid., p. 20.

17. Paul Vallely, *Bad Samaritans: First World Ethics and Third World Debt* (Maryknoll, NY: Orbis Books, 1990), p. 85.

18. *Recolonization or Liberation*, p. 6.

19. Ibid., pp. 7, 8, 24.

20. Harrington, p. 165.

21. Vallely, pp. 149, 192.

22. *Recolonization or Liberation*, p. 20.

23. Vallely, p. 150.

24. *Recolonization or Liberation*, p. 20.

25. See UNICEF, *The State of the World's Children 1989* and *The State of the World's Children 1990* (New York: Oxford University Press, 1989 and 1990).

26. Bello, pp. 60-61.

27. *Recolonization or Liberation*, p. 30.

## Chapter 2

1. Kevin Phillips, *The Politics of Rich and Poor* (New York: Random House, 1990), p. xii.

2. *A Children's Defense Budget, FY 1989: An Analysis of Our Nation's Investment in Children* (Washington, D.C.: Children's Defense Fund, 1988).

3. These six points come from *A Children's Defense Budget, FY 1989*. This report ranked the United States nineteenth in terms of infant mortality, it has since slipped to twenty-second.

4. Bill Nelson, Director of Prison Release Programs for the Volunteers of America, in a talk at Holy Trinity Lutheran Church in Minneapolis, 17 March 1991.

5. *The Oregonian*, 23 May 1991.

6. Phillips, p. 82.

7. Phillips, pp. 76, 78.

8. Phillips, p. 80.

9. Phillips, p. 78.

10. Steve Berg, "Overpaid Top Execs?," *Minneapolis Star Tribune*, 27 July 1991.

11. "Legacy of the Eighties Income Disparity: The Widening Gap," June 1991 newsletter from Minnesota Congressman Martin Olav Sabo.

12. "Winners and Losers: Federal Spending From 1982-86," Jobs With Peace Campaign, 76 Summer Street, Boston, Massachusetts 02110.

13. Phillips, pp. 89-90.

14. "Winners and Losers: Federal Spending From 1982-86."

15. *A Children's Defense Budget, FY 1989*.

16. Nelson.

17. Phillips, p. 90.

18. *Star Tribune*, 1 June 1990.

19. Stephen Labaton, "Revolving Accounts: Are Banks Going Down the Same Path as S. & L.'s?" *The New York Times*, 16 June 1991.

20. Phillips, pp. 90, 91.

21. Phillips, p. 76.

22. David Gordon, quoted in Michael Novak, "The Politics of Envy," *Washington Times*, 7 November 1986.

23. Walden Bello, *Brave New Third World? Strategies for Survival in the Global Economy* (San Francisco: The Institute for Food and Development Policy, 1989), p. 65.

24. Bello, p. 67.

25. Bello, p. 64.

26. Phillips, p. xii.

27. Phillips, p. 141.

28. Phillips, pp. 140-41.

29. J. R. Livingston, "Takeover: Today's Pools," *Philadelphia Inquirer*, 23 November 1986.

30. Phillips, p. 68.

31. Seymour Melman, *The Demilitarized Society* (Montreal: Harvest House, 1988), p. 1.

32. *Star Tribune*, 21 March 1991.

33. Melman, p. 16.

34. "Giving a Little to Save a Lot," *Forbes*, 6 March 1989, p. 39.

35. Quoted in Michael Harrington, *Socialism Past and Future* (New York: Arcade Publishing, 1989), pp. 133-34.

36. *A Children's Defense Budget, FY 1989.*

37. Phillips, pp. 19-20.

38. From the June 1991 newsletter of Minnesota Congressman Martin Olav Sabo.

39. *A Children's Defense Budget, FY 1989*, p. xiii.

## Chapter 3

1. José Comblin, *The Church and the National Security State* (Maryknoll, NY: Orbis Books, 1979), p. 65.

2. Comblin, pp. 64-78.

3. Tom Gibb and Frank Smyth, "El Salvador: Is Peace Possible? A Report on the Prospects for Negotiations and U.S. Policy," Washington Office on Latin America, April 1990.

4. Jon Sobrino, *Companions of Jesus: The Jesuit Martyrs of El Salvador* (Maryknoll, NY: Orbis Books, 1990), pp. 79-80.

5. Jack Nelson-Pallmeyer, *War Against the Poor* (Maryknoll, NY: Orbis Books, 1989), chap. 4.

6. Gibb and Smyth, p. 17.

7. Sobrino, p. xviii.

8. Sobrino, pp. 80-81.

9. Sobrino, p. 14.

10. See for example, testimony of Holly Burkhalter for *America's Watch* to the House Subcommittees on Western Hemisphere Affairs and Human Rights and International Organizations, 31 January 1990.

## Chapter 4

1. José Comblin, *The Church and the National Security State* (Maryknoll, NY: Orbis Books, 1979), p. 65.

2. George Kennan, quoted in Jack Nelson-Pallmeyer, *War Against the Poor: Low-Intensity Conflict and Christian Faith* (Maryknoll, NY: Orbis Books, 1989), p. 5.

3. Quoted in Nelson-Pallmeyer, p. 56.

4. Dwight D. Eisenhower, quoted in Jack A. Nelson, *Hunger for Justice* (Maryknoll, NY: Orbis Books, 1980), pp. 56-57.

5. Ronald Reagan, address before a joint session of Congress on Central America, 27 April 1983.

6. See Noam Chomsky and Edward Herman, *Manufacturing Consent: The Political Economy of the Mass Media* (New York: Pantheon Books, 1988). See also Michael Parenti, *Inventing Reality: The Politics of the Mass Media* (New York: St. Martin's Press, 1986).

7. *EXTRA*, a publication of *Fairness & Accuracy In Reporting*, Special Issue, vol. 4, no. 3, p. 14.

8. Malcolm Browne, *Newsday*, 23 January 1991.

9. Colman McCarthy, talk at Holy Trinity Lutheran Church, 10 March 1991.

10. *EXTRA*, p. 5.

11. *EXTRA*, p. 7.

12. Michael Deaver, quoted in *EXTRA*, p. 14.

13. For more information on the issues behind the Iran-Contra affair write to the Christic Institute, 1324 North Capitol Street, N.W., Washington, D. C. 20002.

14. Bill Moyers, quoted in *Convergence*, a report of the Christic Institute, Winter 1991.

15. This statistic is taken from a written transcript of a Public Affairs Television special, with Bill Moyers, entitled *The Secret Government: The Constitution in Crisis*.

16. "Affidavit of Daniel P. Sheehan," filed on 12 December 1986, p. 5. The affidavit is available from the Christic Institute.

17. Peter Dale Scott and Jonathan Marshall, *Cocaine Politics: Drugs, Armies and the CIA in Central America* (Berkeley: University of California Press, 1991).

18. *Drugs, Law, and Foreign Policy*, a report from the Senate Foreign Relations Committee's subcommittee on Narcotics, Terrorism, and International Operations, April 1989. This is commonly known as the Kerry Committee Report, named after the subcommittee's chair, Senator John Kerry.

19. Bill Teska, "The Covert Connection," *Christian Social Action* (June 1990), p. 16.

20. Gary Sick, "The Election Story of the Decade," *The New York Times*, 15 April 1991. See also, Joel Bleifuss, "Truth: The Last Hostage," *In These Times* (17-23 April 1991).

21. *Star Tribune*, 3 May 1991.

22. Quoted in *Total War Against the Poor* (New York: New York Circus Publications, 1990), p. 133.

23. "U.S., Latin America Sign Secret Defense Plan," *National Catholic Reporter*, 16 December 1988.

### Chapter 5

1. Joseph Gerson and Bruce Birchard, eds., *The Sun Never Sets: Confronting the Network of Foreign U.S. Military Bases* (Boston: South End Press, 1991), pp. 6, 8.

2. Gerson and Birchard, p. 12.

3. Michael Klare, "Facing South: The Pentagon and the Third World in the 1990s," a talk given at the University of Minnesota, 5 October 1990.

4. James Petras, "The Meaning of the New World Order: A Critique," *America*, 11 May 1991, p. 512.

5. Theodore Sorenson, quoted by Klare.

6. Ibid.

7. Colman McCarthy, "Creating Peacetime Profits," *Star Tribune*, 30 April 1990.

8. *National Defense: Journal of the American Defense Preparedness Association* (December 1989).

9. *Marine Corps Gazette* (May 1990), p. 16.

10. Ibid., pp. 17-18.

11. Carl E. Vuono, "Versatile, Deployable, and Lethal: The Strategic Army in the 1990s and Beyond," *Sea Power* (April 1990), p. 61.

12. Michael Levine, quoted in a mailing from the Christic Institute dated 10 May 1991.

13. *Marine Corp Gazette*, p. 19.

14. Ibid.

15. Vuono, pp. 59, 61.

16. *Marine Corps Gazette*, p. 18.

17. Nelson-Pallmeyer, p. ix.

18. *Marine Corps Gazette*, p. 19.

19. Ibid., p. 19.

20. Ibid., p. 20.

21. Ibid., p. 19.

22. Major Mitchell M. Zais, USA, "LIC: Matching Forces and Missions," *Military Review* 66, no. 8 (August 1986), pp. 79, 89.

23. Noel Koch, "Objecting to Reality: The Struggle to Restore U.S. Special Operations Forces," in *Low-Intensity Conflict: The Pattern of*

*Warfare in the Modern World,* ed. Loren B. Thompson (Lexington, MA: Lexington Books, 1989), p. 52.

24. Nelson-Pallmeyer.

25. Nelson-Pallmeyer, chap. 3.

26. Bob Woodward, *The Commanders* (New York: Simon & Schuster, 1991).

27. Bob Woodward, *Veil: The Secret Wars of the CIA* (New York: Simon and Schuster, 1987), pp. 195, 173.

28. Penny Lernoux, *People of God* (New York: Viking Press, 1989), pp. 373-374.

29. Michael Klare, "The Evolution of U.S. Doctrine for Low-Intensity Conflict," a paper produced for the MacArthur Interdisciplinary Program on Peace and International Cooperation at the University of Minnesota, October 1990, p. 1.

30. General Gray, *Marine Corps Gazette,* p. 19.

31. Michael Klare, "The Evolution of U.S. Doctrine," p. 2.

32. General Gray, p. 19.

33. Ibid.

34. Ibid.

## Chapter 6

1. *Marine Corp Gazette* (March 1990), p. 17.

2. Michael Klare, "Facing South: The Pentagon and the Third World in the 1990s," a talk given at the University of Minnesota, 5 October 1990.

3. April Glaspie, quoted by Christopher Hitchens, "Why We Are Stuck in the Sand?," *Harpers Magazine,* January 1991, p. 73.

4. John Kelly, from U.S. State Department transcript of press conference, 24 July, 1990, pp. 4-5.

5. *Z Magazine,* April 1991, p. 53.

6. *St. Petersburg Times,* 6 January 1991.

7. Andrew and Leslie Cockburn, *Dangerous Liaison: The Inside Story of the U.S.-Israeli Covert Relationship* (New York: Harper Collins, 1991), p. 353.

8. Ibid., p. 354.

9. *Wall Street Journal,* 7 December 1990.

10. Doyle McManus and Robin Wright, "Events Imperil Bush's Strategy," *Star Tribune,* 22 February 1991.

11. *Newsweek,* 4 March 1991, p. 51.

12. "Eventually There Can Only Be an Arab Solution," *Middle East Report* (March-April 1991), p. 10.

13. Ibid.

14. Ibid., p. 9.

15. Ibid.

16. James Webb, *The Washington Times*, 14 January 1991.

17. Henry Gonzales, H.R. 34, *Resolution of Impeachment of President George Herbert Walker Bush*, 102d Congress, 1st session, introduced into the U.S. House of Representatives on 16 January 1991.

18. *Middle East Report* (March-April 1991), p. 9.

19. Ibid.

20. Gonzalez.

21. Richard Armitage, *The Washington Times*, 16 August 1990.

22. Richard Reid, quoted in "5 Million Children Gulf Crisis Victims," *AL-AHRAM* (a weekly newspaper from Cairo, Egypt), 28 March 1991.

23. "Higher Death Rate Found in Iraq Children," *Star Tribune*, 22 May 1991.

24. H. Jack Geiger, quoted in "Death in Slow Motion: Famine and Disease Stalk Iraq," *Star Tribune*, 17 April 1991.

25. Ibid.

26. Lance Morrow, "A Moment for the Dead," *Time* (April 1, 1991).

27. Geiger.

28. *Star Tribune*, 3 March 1991.

29. Norman Schwarzkopf, quoted in *Star Tribune*, 1 April 1991.

30. *Star Tribune*, 4 April 1991.

31. *Z Magazine* (January 1991), p. 55.

32. Beinin, "Origins of the Gulf War," talk given at the University of Wisconsin in Madison, 30 November 1990.

33. United Nation's Development Program report, quoted in *The Oregonian*, 23 May 1991.

34. David Broder, quoted in *Star Tribune*, 15 May 1991.

35. Colin Powell, quoted in Klare, "Facing South."

36. James Petras, "The Meaning of the New World Order: A Critique," *America* (May 11, 1991), p. 512.

37. Michael Klare, "High-Death Weapons of the Gulf War," *The Nation* (3 June, 1991).

38. Andrew and Leslie Cockburn, pp. 354-355.

39. Ibid., p. 355.

40. Otis Pike, "Different Services But Only One War," quoted in the *Star Tribune*, 21 February 1991.

41. John McCain, "The Need for Strategy in the New Postwar Era," *Armed Forces Journal* (January 1990), p. 46.

42. *Z Magazine* (February 1991), p. 56.

43. Ibid.

44. Thomas L. Friedman, "NATO's Difficult Career Change," *The New York Times*, 9 June 1991.

45. Klare, "Facing South."

46. *Newsweek* (March 4, 1991), p. 51.

47. *Star Tribune*, 9 May 1991.

### Chapter 7

1. Lester Brown, et al., *State of the World 1990* (New York: W. W. Norton, 1990), p. xv. The analysis in this chapter draws heavily on Worldwatch Institute reports from 1990 and 1991. I have listed exact pages only in the case of direct quotations.

2. Ibid.

3. Herman E. Daly and John B. Cobb, Jr., *For the Common Good: Redirecting the Economy Toward Community, the Environment, and a Sustainable Future* (Boston: Beacon Press, 1989), p. 13.

4. Lester Brown, *State of the World 1990*, pp. 3, 5.

5. Lester Brown, *State of the World 1991* (New York: W. W. Norton, 1991), pp. 4-5.

6. Alan Durning, *State of the World 1990*, p. 135.

7. Lloyd Timberlake, *Africa in Crisis: The Causes, the Cures of Environmental Bankruptcy* (Philadelphia: New Society Publishers/International Institute for Environment and Development, 1986), p. 9.

8. Durning, pp. 135-36.

9. Durning, pp. 144-45.

10. Timberlake, p. 133.

11. Durning, p. 144.

12. *State of the World 1991*, p. 171.

13. Ibid., p. 151.

14. Durning, p. 144.

15. Durning, p. 153.

16. *State of the World 1991*, p. 174.

17. Ibid., p. 144.

18. Ibid., p. 176.

19. Ibid., p. 177.

20. Sandra Postel and Christopher Flavin, *State of the World 1991*, p. 188.

21. *State of the World 1991*, p. 180.

22. Ibid., p. 181.

23. Ibid., pp. 188-89.

24. *State of the World 1990*, p. 190.

25. Ibid., pp. 187-88.

26. *State of the World 1991*, p. 3.

27. Ibid., p. 18.

28. Ibid., pp. 18-19.

29. Ibid., p. 188.

30. *State of the World 1990*, p. 16.

31. Michael Renner, *State of the World 1991*, p. 132.

32. "Saddam Hussein's Inferno," *The New York Times*, 9 June 1991.

33. *State of the World 1990*, p. 176.

34. Jane Holtz Kay, "The Road to Nowhere," *The New York Times*, 9 June 1991.

35. "Love Canals in the Making," *Time*, 20 May 1991.

## Chapter 8

1. Marcus J. Borg, *Jesus: A New Vision* (San Francisco: Harper & Row, 1987), p. 195.

2. Ched Myers, *Binding the Strong Man: A Political Reading of Mark's Story of Jesus* (Maryknoll, NY: Orbis Books, 1988), p. 123.

3. Myers, p. 124.

4. Myers, p. 419.

5. Josephus, quoted in Myers, p. 215.

6. Myers, p. 191.

7. Myers, pp. 51-52.

8. Bill Wylie Kellermann, *Seasons of Faith and Conscience* (Maryknoll, NY: Orbis Books, 1991), p. 29.

9. Borg, p. 91.

10. Borg, p. 91.

11. Myers, pp. 75-76.

12. Myers, pp. 142-43.

13. Borg, p. 100.

14. Borg, p. 180.

15. Kellermann, p. 172.

16. Myers, p. 428.

17. Myers, p. 427.

18. Myers, p. 250.

## Chapter 9

1. *Sojourners* (February-March 1991), p. 5.

2. Edgar R. Trexler, "War Is Not the Answer," *The Lutheran* 30 (January 1991), p. 50.

3. Joan Chittister, "Are We Becoming What We Hate?," *Sojourners* (April 1991), p. 4.

4. "A Call to the Churches," *Sojourners* (April 1991), p. 13.

5. Quoted in Anthony A. Parker, "An Opportunity in Crisis: Black Leadership and the New World Order," *Sojourners* (April 1991), p. 19.

6. Coretta Scott King, quoted in Parker.

7. Benjamin F. Chavis, Jr., quoted in Parker.

8. Parker, pp. 19-20.

9. Parker, p. 21.

10. Jeanie Wylie-Kellermann, "Keeping the Faith," *Detroit Metro Times*, 5-11 December 1990, pp. 10-12.

11. Trexler, p. 50.

12. "A Call to the Churches," p. 13.

13. "Renewing Covenants," *One World* [a monthly magazine of the World Council of Churches], no. 155 (May 1990), p. 6.

14. Myers, p. 421.

15. A large number of grass-roots organizations, together with the National Council of Churches, initiated a process of grass-roots discernment, community formation, and political action around 1992, the 500-year anniversary of the conquest of the Americas. For information contact National Council of Churches/1992 Kairos USA, 475 Riverside Drive, Room 572, NYC, NY 10115.

16. Jon Sobrino, conversations with the author.

17. Kellermann, *Seasons of Faith and Conscience*, p. 18.

18. Myers, p. 384.

19. Kellermann, *Seasons of Faith and Conscience*, p. 19.

20. Borg, p. 139.

21. Kellermann, *Seasons of Faith and Conscience*, pp. 17-18.

22. Hippolytus, quoted in Kellermann, *Seasons of Faith and Conscience*, p. 18.

23. "Rome Loses Taste for Just-War," *National Catholic Reporter*, 2 August 1991.

24. Aldous Huxley, *Brave New World* (New York: Harper & Row, 1969), p. 248.

# Index

al-Ashtal, Ambassador Abdalleh, 78-79
*America's Watch*, 40
Amnesty International: "El Salvador: Killings, Torture and Disappearances," *xii*; on Kuwait, *xii*; "Saudi Arabia: Detention without Trial of Suspected Political Prisoners," *xii*; "Saudi Arabia: Torture, Detention, and Arbitrary Arrests," *xii*
Annual Convention of National Religious Broadcasters, the, 134
Arab summit, proposed, 74
Arctic National Wildlife Refuge, the, 110
*Armed Forces Journal*, 90
Armitage, Richard, 81
Authority, religious, Jesus and, 122-23
Baker, James, 73, 80
Bani-Sadr, President, *My Turn to Speak: Iran, the Revolution and Secret Deals with the U.S.*, 52
Baptism, Jesus', 131
Beinin, Joel: on the new world order, 2; on petro-dollars, 86
Bello, Walden, 24-25
Bonhoeffer, Dietrich, 156
Boren, Senator David, 56-57, 58

Borg, Marcus: on American values, 114; on Jesus' murder, 124; on nonviolence, 152-53; on "the politics of holiness," 120, 121
*Brave New World* (Huxley), *vii*, *xiii*, 1, 94, 106, 155
Broder, David, 87
Brown, Lester, 97-98
Browne, Malcolm, 47
Bush, George: to the Annual Convention of National Religious Broadcasters, 134-36; Billy Graham and, 134; the Cold War and, 55; David Frost and, 6-7; Gulf crisis and, 68, 72; on Iraqi troops in Kuwait, 76; military confrontation and, 77; on the new world order, *ix*, *x*; popularity of, *viii*, 110-11; on Saddam Hussein, *viii-ix*
"A Call to the Churches," 137, 141
Capital flight, 15
Capitalism and socialism, economic shortcomings of, 95-96
Casey, William, 49, 68
Central American foreign policy, U.S., *ix-xiii*
Central Intelligence Agency, the, 44
Chavis, Rev. Benjamin F., Jr., 139

*Chicago Tribune, The,* 90

*Children in Need* (The Committee for Economic Development), 30

Chittister, Joan, 137

Christic Institute, the, 49, 50

Church, the: the National Security State and, 46; the new world order and, 133-57; prophetic role of, 154-55; tasks of, 146-55

*The Church and the National Security State* (Comblin), 34

Church, Senator Frank, 45

Civil disobedience, Jesus and, 124, 126

*Cocaine Politics* (Scott and Marshall), 50-51

Cockburn, Andrew and Leslie, 76, 88

Cold War, the: end of, 55-70, 95; the Third World and, 3-5

Coldwell Banker Real Estate Group, the, 26

Comblin, José: *The Church and the National Security State,* 34; on National Security States, 42

*The Commanders* (Woodward), 68

Committee for Economic Development, the, *Children in Need: Investment Strategies for the Economically Disadvantaged,* 30

Communities, alternative, 124-25, 146-48

Conference of American Armies, the, 52-53

Congressional Budget Office, the, 21

Contras, the, 68

Council on Competitiveness, the, 27

Cross, the, 129, 130

Daly, Herman E., and Cobb, John B., Jr., 95-96

Deaver, Michael, 48

*Defense News,* 59

Deficits, U.S. budget, 21, 23

Democracy, Salvadoran, 36

*Diario Latino,* 40

Disciples, the, failure of, 128-29

Discipleship: obstacles to, 128-32; tasks of, 114-32

Domestic problems, U.S., 87

*Drugs, Law, and Foreign Policy* (Kerry), 51

Drug trade, the, 50-52

Drug war, the, 61-62

Durning, Alan: on debt burdens, 101; on poverty, 98, 99, 100, 102

Early Church, the, nonviolence and, 152-53

Economic: decline, U.S., 23-30; devastation, Gulf War, 82; growth, 104; influence, U.S., 57-58; policies, U.S., domestic, 20-23; policies, U.S., foreign, 1-17; power, 91; sanctions of Iraq, 75-76

Economic Recovery Tax Act (1981), 21

Economy, U.S., 18-32

Ecumenical Coalition for Economic Justice, the: on export emphasis, 14-16; on multinational corporations, 11; on SAPS, 12-13, 16-17

Eisenhower, Dwight D., 42, 44, 45, 46

*El Diario,* 46

Elites: national and international, 7-8; third-world, 16

Ellacuría, Ignacio, 39, 52

El Salvador: as a National Security State, 35-41; *Processo* on "democratic process," 6; religious persecution in, 40-41; U.S. military aid to, *x*

"El Salvador: Is Peace Possible?" (The Washington Office on Latin America), 38

"El Salvador: Killings, Torture and Disappearances" (Amnesty International), *xii*

Employment, 105-106

Energy efficiency, 104-105

Environment, the, 94-113

European Economic Community, the, 24

Executive power, U.S., 81

Extinction of plants and animals, 96

Fahd, King, 74

*Fairness and Accuracy In Reporting*, 47-48

Faith and empire, conflict between, 115-18

Faribundo Marti National Liberation Front (FMLN), 38, 39

Federal Deposit Insurance Corporation, the, 23

Fine, Dr. Jonathan, 82

Fitzwater, Marlin, *vii*

*Forbes*, 28

Forces, excessive, U.S., 84

Foreign policy, U.S.: Central American, *ix-xiii*; drug trade and, 50-52; U.N. resolutions and, *xi*; World Court and, *xi*

Free trade, 10

Friedman, Thomas, 91

Frost, David, 6-7

Geiger, Dr. H. Jack, 82

Geneva Conventions, the, 83

Glaspie, April, 72-73

Global warming, 97

Gordon, David, 23

Gonzales, Congressman Henry, 80-81

Government Accounting Office, the, 29

Graham, Billy, 134

Gray, General A. M.: on low-intensity conflict, 69; on the Middle East, 70; on the military sector, 64-65; on narco-terrorism, 61, 62; on social turmoil, 63; on third-world dangers, 63-64; on weapons proliferation, 69-70

*Green Book* (House Ways and Means Committee), 21

"Green taxes," 106

Gulf War, the, 71-93: causes of, 72-81; the Church and, 136-42; Church leaders on, *vii*; effects of, 81-83; global environmental crisis and, 109-12; institutional imperatives toward, 88; media coverage of, 47-48; moral legitimacy of, 5; the peace dividend and, 95; principle reasons for, 85-92; religious support of, 138; U.S. National Security Establishment and, 35; U.S. war crimes during, 83-84

Gumbleton, Bishop Thomas, 140

Harrington, Michael, 10

Healing, Jesus and, 123

Heller, Jean, 76

"High Crimes and Misdemeanors" (Moyers), 49-50

Hippolytus, on baptism, 153

Holiness, politics of, 120, 121

House Ways and Means Committee, *Green Book*, 21

Human development index, the, 86

Hussein, King, 74

Hussein, Saddam, 76, 77

Huxley, Aldous, *Brave New World*, *vii, xiii,* 1, 94, 155

Iacocca, Lee, 29

Indebtedness, third-world, 13-14

International market economy, poverty and, 5

International Monetary Fund, the, 117; economic policing function of, *xiii*; environmental destruction and, 100-101; international economy and, 7; policies, 12-17

Interservice rivalry, U.S., 89-90

Iran-Contra scandal, the, 45, 48-50

Iraq: economic sanctions of, 75-76; invasion of Kuwait, causes of, 73-74

Japanese economy, the, 24-25

Jesus: civil disobedience and, 124; religious authorities and, 117-24

Jewish-Roman War (66-70 C.E.), 119

Jewish Temple, the, 119-21

Jimenez, Perez, 44

John the Baptist, 116

Joint Chiefs of Staff, the, 66

Josephus, 116

Kay, Jane Holtz, 110

Kellermann, Bill Wylie: on choice, 128; on Jesus' death, 148-49; on Passover commerce, 120; on sacrament, 152

Kelly, John, 73

Kennan, George, 43

Kerala, India, 101

Kerry, Senator John, *Drugs, Law, and Foreign Policy*, 51

King, Coretta Scott, 139

Klare, Michael: on the Cold War, 55, 70; on the Gulf War, 72, 88; on low-intensity conflict, 69; on the National Security Establishment, 59; on U.S. military power, 91

Koch, Noel, 66

Kramer, Michael, "Read My Ships," 1

Kuwait, Amnesty International report on, *xii*

*La Civilta Catolica*, 153

Land ownership, the World Bank and, 8

Levine, Michael, 61

Liberation theology, 52

Lifestyles, less consumptive, 106-107

Liman, Arthur, 49

London *Financial Times*, the, 90

*Los Angeles Times*, the, 77

Low-intensity conflict, 66-69

*The Lutheran*, 137, 140

McCain, Senator John, 90

McCarthy, Colman, 47

McCarthy, Joseph, 45

*Manchester Guardian Weekly*, The, 71

*Marine Corps Gazette*, "On the Corps' Continuing Role," 60

Mark, Gospel of, 114-32

Markets, role of, 10

Marquand, Daniel, 71

Martin-Baro, Ignacio, 36, 39, 40

Medellín cartel, the, 51

Media, the, 46-48

Melman, Seymour, 27

Mexico free-trade agreement, 111-12

*Middle East Report*, 78

Military-industrial complex, the, 42, 45, 46

Military spending, U.S., 21

Minneapolis *Star Tribune*, The, *viii*

Mitchell, Senator George, 21

Morrow, Lance, 82-83

Moyers, Bill, "High Crimes and Misdemeanors," 49-50

Moynihan, Senator Patrick, 23

Mubarek, President, 74

Multinational corporations, 10-11

Myers, Ched: on the cross, 130; on Jesus' death, 149; on Jesus' nonviolence, 130-31; on Mark, 115-16, 117-18, 121, 122; on radical discipleship, 146

Myths, destructive, 125-28

*My Turn to Speak* (Bani-Sadr), 52

Narco-terrorism, 61, 62

*National Catholic Reporter*, The, 53, 153

*National Defense: Journal of the American Defense Preparedness Association*, 59-60

National Emergency African-American Leadership Summit on the Gulf War, the, 138-39

National Security Act, the (1947), 43

National Security Council, the, 43-44

National Security Establishment, U.S., 42-46, 55-70

National Security State, U.S., 42-54: characteristics of, 34; the Church and, 46; doctrine of, 33-41; formation of, 42-46; the media and, 46-48; signs of, 46-53

Nelson-Pallmeyer, Jack, *War Against the Poor: Low-Intensity Conflict and Christian Faith, ix,* 36

Neuhaus, Richard John, 68

*Newsday*, on excessive U.S. force, 84

*Newsweek*: on economic power, 91; "A Wrinkle in the New World Order," 77-78

New world order, the, 56: George Bush on, *ix, x*; Joel Beinin on, 2; key objectives of, 3; National Security State doctrine and, 33-41

*New York Times*, The, 91, 109-10

Nonviolence: the Church and, 151-53; Jesus' commitment to, 130-31

Noriega, Manuel, 51

North, Oliver, 49

Odria, Manuel, 44

Oil, importance of, 85-86

Patriotism, idolatrous, 134-36

Paul, James, 78-79

"Peace dividend," the, 34, 60, 61, 69, 95

Persecution, religious, in El Salvador, 40-41

Petras, James, 57-58, 87

*Philadelphia Inquirer*, The, 26

Phillips, Kevin: *The Politics of Rich and Poor*, 18; on Reagan and Bush, 19; on speculation, 26; on tax reforms, 25; on U.S. budget deficit, 23

Physicians for Human Rights, 82, 83

Pike, Otis, 89-90

Poindexter, John, 49

*The Politics of Rich and Poor* (Phillips), 18

Pollution, air, 96-97

Poor, the: first-century, 119; third-world, 7-9

Population growth, 97-98, 101

Postel, Sandra, and Flavin, Christopher, 104

Poverty: environment and, 101-102; international market economy and, 5; third-world, 7-17; U.S., 19-23

Powell, General Colin, 68, 87

Power, economic, 91

President's Commission on Industrial Competitiveness, the, 28

*Processo*, 6

Productivity, environmental impact on, 97-98

"Read My Ships" (Kramer), 1

Reagan, Ronald: presidential directives and, 50; U.S. policies in Central America and, 44

Recycling, 105

Reforestation, 104

Reid, Richard, 82

Renner, Michael, 109

"Rethinking National Security" (Sorenson), 58

Richard, Pablo, 4

Risk taking, the Church and, 150-53

Romero, Archbishop Oscar, 33, 34, 41, 117

*St. Petersburg Times*, The, 76

Saudi Arabia: human development index and, 86; Iraqi threat to, 75-76

"Saudi Arabia: Detention without Trial of Suspected Political Prisoners" (Amnesty International), *xii*

"Saudi Arabia: Torture, Detention, and Arbitrary Arrests" (Amnesty International), *xii*

Savings and loan industry, the, 22-23

Schwartzkopf, General H. Norman, 84-85, 93, 133, 134

Scott, Peter Dale, and Marshall, Jonathan, *Cocaine Politics: Drugs, Armies and the CIA in Central America*, 50-51

Sick, Gary, 52

Sobrino, Jon, 17: on oppression, 147-48; *Sojourners*, 33; on state-sponsored terrorism, 40; on third-world poverty, 5

Sol, Jorge, 12

Solar energy, 103-104

Sorenson, Theodore, "Rethinking National Security," 58

Soviet peace initiative, the, 77-78

Soviet threat, effects of, 56

Spirit, the, discernment of, 127-28

*Spokane Chronicle*, The, 59

Sri Lanka, 86

*State of the World 1990* (Worldwatch Institute), 94, 95, 96, 110, 113

*State of the World 1991* (Worldwatch Institute), 96

Structural adjustment programs (IMF), 12-17, 100-101

Surrogate forces, 67-68

Sustainability, environmental, 102, 103-107

Tax reforms, U.S., 20-21, 25

Tax resistance, the Church and, 151

Taylor, General Maxwell, 63

Temple curtain, the, 131

Teska, Bill, 51-52

Third world, the: the Cold War and, 3-5; environmental crisis and, 98-102; indebtedness, 13-14; Pablo Richard on, 4; poverty, exploitation of, 7-9; U.S.

economic policies and, 1-17; U.S. military and, 62-66

Timberlake, Lloyd, 98-99

Tithing, the Jewish Temple and, 119-20

*Trained and Ready in an Era of Change* (Vuono), 69

Transfiguration, the, 131

Trexler, Edgar, 137, 140

Twain, Mark, *The War Poem*, 71, 133-34

UNICEF, on SAP austerity measures, 16

United Nations: Charter, the, 79; Commission on Trade and Development, the, 11; Development Program, the, 86; Resolution 678, 79, 80; resolutions, U.S. and, *xi*

United States economy, the, 18-32, 57-58

United States military, the: Cold War and, 59-61; the drug war and, 61-62; low-intensity conflict and, 66-69; power and, 90-91; spending cuts and, 59-60; surrogate forces and, 67-68; third world and, 62-66

United States Security State, the, 35, 42-54

United States 1980 presidential election, the, 52

Vallely, Paul, 15

"Vietnam syndrome," the, *viii*, 67, 68, 69

Viorst, Milton, 73

Vuono, Carl E.: on narco-terrorism, 61; on third-world dangers, 62-63; *Trained and Ready in an Era of Change*, 69

*Wall Street Journal*, The, 77

*War Against the Poor* (Nelson-Pallmeyer), *ix*, 36

War crimes, U.S., 83-84

*The War Poem* (Twain), 71, 133-34

Washington Office on Latin America, the, 53-54; "El Salvador: Is Peace Possible?" 38

Wealth, U.S., redistribution of, 19

Wealth transfer, 7-17, 98

Weapons proliferation, 69-70

Webb, James, 79-80

Woodward, Bob, *The Commanders*, 68

World Bank, the, 8

World Council of Churches convocation on Justice, Peace and the Integrity of Creation, 144-45

World Court, U.S. and, *xi*

Worldwatch Institute, the, *xiv-xv*, 102-103; reports of, 107-109; *State of the World 1990*, 94, 95, 96, 110, 113; *State of the World 1991*, 96

Zimmermann, Peter, 76